ORTHO'S All About

Herbs

Written by Maggie Oster

Meredith® Books
Des Moines, Iowa

P9-DFU-991

Ortho® Books
An imprint of Meredith® Books

All About Herbs
Editor: Marilyn K. Rogers
Technical Consultants: Madalene Hill, Gwen Barclay
Art Director: Tom Wegner
Copy Chief: Catherine Hamrick
Copy and Production Editor: Terri Fredrickson
Contributing Copy Editors: Cynthia S. Howell, Ed Malles, Diane Witosky
Contributing editor: Leona H. Openshaw
Contributing Proofreaders: Kathy Roth Eastman, Mary Pas, Steve Hallam
Contributing Map Illustrator: Jana Fothergill
Contributing Prop/Photo Stylists: Peggy Johnston, Mary Klingamon, Diane Munkel
Projects sewed by Margaret Sindelar
Indexer: Don Glassman
Electronic Production Coordinator: Paula Forest
Editorial and Design Assistants: Kathleen Stevens, Karen Schirm
Production Director: Douglas M. Johnston
Production Manager: Pam Kvitne
Assistant Prepress Manager: Marjorie J. Schenkelberg

Additional Editorial Contributions from
   Art Rep Services
Director: Chip Nadeau
Designer: lk Design

Meredith® Books
Editor in Chief: James D. Blume
Design Director: Matt Strelecki
Managing Editor: Gregory H. Kayko
Executive Ortho Editor: Benjamin W. Allen

Director, Sales & Marketing, Retail: Michael A. Peterson
Director, Sales & Marketing, Special Markets: Rita McMullen
Director, Sales & Marketing, Home & Garden Center Channel: Ray Wolf
Director, Operations: George A. Susral

Vice President, General Manager: Jamie L. Martin

Meredith Publishing Group
President, Publishing Group: Christopher M. Little
Vice President, Consumer Marketing & Development: Hal Oringer

Meredith Corporation
Chairman and Chief Executive Officer: William T. Kerr

Chairman of the Executive Committee: E.T. Meredith III

On the cover: Borage, thyme, scented geranium and rose. Photo by Jerry Pavia.

All of us at Ortho® Books are dedicated to providing you with the information and ideas you need to enhance your home and garden. We welcome your comments and suggestions about this book. Write to us at:
   Meredith Corporation
   Ortho Books
   1716 Locust St.
   Des Moines, IA 50309–3023

If you would like more information on other Ortho products, call 800-225-2883 or visit us at www.ortho.com

Copyright © 1999 The Scotts Company
Some text, photography, and artwork copyright © 1999 Meredith Corporation
All rights reserved. Printed in the United States of America.
First Edition. Printing Number and Year:
   10 9 8 7 6   03 02 01 00
Library of Congress Catalog Card Number: 98-66920
ISBN: 0-89721-420-X

Thanks to
Janet Anderson, Carol Boker, Laura Davenport, Michelle George, Melissa George, Gina M. Hale, Colleen Johnson, Aimee Reiman, Mary Irene Swartz; The Farmhouse, Grimes, Iowa

Photographers
(Photographers credited may retain copyright © to the listed photographs.)
L= Left, R= Right, C= Center, B= Bottom, T= Top
Cathy Wilkinson Barash: p. 85B
Karen Bussolini/Positive Images: p. 13T
David Cavagnaro: p. 5TL, 6BR, 21, 57B, 61B, 64B, 67B, 70T, 86B, 88B
Rosalind Creasy: p. 6BL, 63T, 66T, 83T;
R. Todd Davis: p. 71T;
Alan & Linda Detrick: p. 7CL, 51, 63B
Thomas E. Eltzroth: p. 7TR
Derek Fell: p. 58T, 77B, 83B, 87B
Steven Foster: p. 44T, 72B
John Glover: p. 5TR, 13BR, 25TL, 27T, 28B, 30BL, 31T, 33T, 34B, 37C, 38B, 57T, 61T, 76T, 84T, 87T, 88T, 89B, 90B, 91B
David Goldberg: p. 4, 15BL,BR, 16, 19BR,CR, 22T, 23B
Jeff Gracz: p. 92T
Harry Haralambou/Positive Images: p. 74T
Marcus Harpur: p. 7BL
Jerry Harpur: p. 13BL, 25BR, 27B, 29T,BR, 32T, 50R, 52C
Jerry Howard/Positive Images: p. 79T
Bill Johnson: p. 86T
Dency Kane: p. 38T
Lynn Karlin: p. 69T, 75B, 81T, 91T
Dwight R. Kuhn: p. 6TR
Lee Lockwood/Positive Images: p. 62T
Janet Loughrey: p. 79B, 89T
Allan Mandell: p. 14T, 25TR, 82B
Charles Mann: p. 28T, 58C, 59T, 60, 64T, 67T, 71B, 73B, 74B, 76B, 80B, 85T, 92B;
Bryan McCay: p. 12, 20, 29BL
Clive Nichols/Mark Brown: p. 26
Maggie Oster: p. 33B, 62B, 65, 68B, 90T
Jerry Pavia: p. 6LC, 50L, 59B, 66B, 69B, 72T, 75T, 78T, 80T, 81C,B, 82T, 84B
Joanne Pavia: p. 77T
Susan A. Roth: p. 6TL,CR, 30T, 31B, 34T, 36TL, 37TR, 43B, 78B,
Richard Shiell: p. 7TL, 36B
Pam Spaulding/Positive Images: p. 68T
Steve Struse: p. 5BL, 7CR,BR, 19TL,TR, 22B, 23T,C, 24, 35B, 39, 40B, 41T, 42TL,CL,BL, 45, 52T, 53, 54, 55
Michael S. Thompson: p. 37B, 44C, 52B
Connie Toops: p. 58B, 73T

Note to the Readers:
Due to differing conditions, tools, and individual skills, Meredith Corporation assumes no responsibility for any damages, injuries suffered, or losses incurred as a result of following the information published in this book. Always read and observe all of the safety precautions provided by manufacturers of any tools, equipment, or supplies, and follow all accepted safety procedures.

The book is intended to provide you with information about growing and using herbs. It is not intended to be a medical guide or serve as a substitute for advice from your doctor. Every person's health needs are unique. Diagnosis and treatment must be done through a health care professional. Please consult a doctor for all your health care needs.

LIVING WITH HERBS

Herbs' luscious flavors enhance your meals. Their beneficial properties improve your health and well-being. And they're the backbone of fragrantly beautiful decorations for your home. Tend them well so they flourish in your garden.

Fill your life with herbs. They will bring beauty to your yard and luscious flavors to your meals. Some can improve your health and appearance. Others fill your home with fragrance.

More than a thousand plants are considered herbs, so there are lots of candidates for your garden. In this book, you'll learn to recognize, grow, and use more than 70 of the most flavorful, beneficial, and fragrant herbs.

So what exactly is an herb? More than 12 centuries ago, Emperor Charlemagne, who compelled his citizens to grow herbs, answered this question by saying: "An herb is the friend of physicians and the praise of cooks."

Not much has changed since then, except that the definition has expanded from the fields of medicine and cooking to include plants valued for their household, fragrant, or economic uses. Because herbs have played a part in civilizations since the earliest times, they also provide entertainment through their wealth of history and folklore.

And how is the word herb pronounced? Derived from the Latin word herba, for vegetation or green plant, the letter h was originally pronounced. The h was dropped as the romance languages—Italian, Spanish, and French—evolved and even was omitted in the spelling for awhile. By the Middle Ages, the h was in place again, both in the written and spoken word in England. The French, however, chose to keep the h muted. Today, the British sound the h, while most Americans do not.

Ultimately, how you pronounce "herb" is less important than including them in your garden and home.

The flavors and aromas of herbs intertwine with all foods, from appetizers to vegetables, breads, soups, salads, main courses, drinks, and desserts.

In the garden, herbs contribute beauty and fragrance with their foliage and flowers. Herbs can be planted in areas designed specifically for them or used throughout the garden, mixed in among other plants.

For health, herbs provide essential minerals and vitamins, and they can be used to heal a wide variety of ailments, and in maintaining skin, hair, and nails.

For fragrance, herbs are unsurpassed. The therapeutic scent of herbs soothes bodies and spirits, while herbal crafts make homes more beautiful.

SUCCESSFULLY GROWING AND USING HERBS

Growing and using herbs are not particularly difficult, but to derive the most pleasure, benefit, and success from your effort, there are seven key points to consider.

Know your herbs. Minimize mistakes and confusion by knowing—before planting it in your garden—how each herb grows, the conditions under which it needs to grow, and how to use the herb after you harvest it Take an herb book with you when plant shopping, then keep it handy in your home. Label plants in the garden and dried herbs stored in the pantry.

Provide the right conditions. Herbs grow best when light, soil, drainage, and climatic conditions meet each herb's requirements for healthy growth.

Provide the proper care. Watering, pruning, pinching, harvesting, and providing winter protection for plants help ensure healthy, vigorous herbs.

Experiment in the kitchen. Don't let culinary herbs intimidate you. If an herb is new to you, nibble on it; then let your imagination fly with all the possibilities it can bring to your meals. Start with small quantities until you feel sure of yourself. And remember, it's hard to fail with fresh herbs.

For healing, use the right herb in the proper manner. Herbs can be potent or benign. To avoid problems and successfully treat a disorder, use only the herbs suggested for the ailment at the recommended dosage.

Use herbs throughout the home. Besides filling your kitchen and medicine cabinet, herbs bring fragrance and beauty to every room of the house. Use them in potpourris, wreaths, or other aromatic crafts.

Enjoy the beauty of herbs. For centuries, gardeners have enjoyed the peaceful quality herbs impart to gardens. Take time to stroll and sit among them to regenerate your spirit.

PLANT TYPES

When deciding which herbs to grow and how best to use them in the landscape, it's helpful to know something about the many different types of plants and their growth habits.

Annuals and biennials
Annuals germinate, grow, flower, and die in one growing season, while biennials germinate and grow vegetatively the first season, go dormant over winter in cold areas, then flower the second growing season before dying. Basil (Ocimum basilicum) is an annual herb.

Trees
Woody plants usually have a single main stem but sometimes have two or three stems. Branches form well above the ground. Leaves may be deciduous or evergreen. Examples of trees that are herbs are willow (Salix species) and linden (Tilia species).

Vines
Vines are plants with woody or herbaceous stems that climb supports, either by twining or by means of suckers or tendrils. Many vines sprawl and must be supported. Honeysuckle (Lonicera species) is an example of a vine with herbal uses.

Shrubs
Woody plants are shorter than trees, with multiple stems and many branches starting near the base of the plant. Leaves may be deciduous or evergreen. A shrub that is an herb is elder (Sambucus species).

Herbaceous perennials
Plants that usually die back to the ground in winter, then send out new growth in spring are perennial. Most have soft, herbaceous stems, but some develop woody stems. Sage (Salvia officinalis) is an example of a perennial herb.

Other herbs
Many herbs do not fit into the other categories. These include ferns, mosses, seaweed, horsetail (left), and some algae. Fungi, which are no longer considered plants, also may serve as herbs. Herbal fungi include yeasts.

PLANT PARTS

Not all parts of an herb have herbal properties. Be sure to choose the correct part for the herb in question.

Roots

These below-ground structures anchor plants in the soil, absorb water and nutrients, and serve as storage organs. They may be thin and fibrous or thick and woody. Other forms include bulbs, corms, and tubers. Rhizomes, runners, and stolons are horizontal stems, not roots. One herb that's a root is horseradish.

Leaves and Stems

Other than a few bacteria, plants are the only organisms that produce their own food. This occurs in the leaves, and they are the primary source of the chemicals we seek from herbs. Stems support plants and transport nutrients. Herbaceous stems are a source of fibers for crafts. The herb in the photo above is bay (Laurus nobilis).

Flowers

Plants reproduce through flowers. The petals, with their color and scent, attract insects that aid pollination. Many flowers contain male and female organs. Roses are flowers we use as herbs.

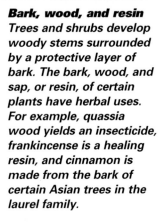

Bark, wood, and resin

Trees and shrubs develop woody stems surrounded by a protective layer of bark. The bark, wood, and sap, or resin, of certain plants have herbal uses. For example, quassia wood yields an insecticide, frankincense is a healing resin, and cinnamon is made from the bark of certain Asian trees in the laurel family.

Seeds, fruits, and nuts

After fertilization, plants form seeds. Each seed contains a store of food and a dormant embryo. Seeds are a major source of the world's food and oil. Some plants, such as the dill at left, produce "naked" or exposed seed. Others develop seed in a fleshy fruit. A nut is a woody fruit.

Essential oils

Essential oils are the concentrated, aromatic (volatile) oils of plants. Depending on the plant, these may come from any plant part. Besides providing fragrance, essential oils also may flavor or heal. Lavender provides an important herbal essential oil.

COMMON HERBS AND THEIR USES

Name	Parts Used	In the Kitchen	In the Home and Garden	For Health and Beauty
Aloe *Aloe vera*	Leaves			Minor burns, wounds, insect bites, dry skin, itchy scalp, dandruff
Angelica *Angelica archangelica*	Leaves, stems, seeds, roots	Desserts, acid fruits, liqueurs, crystallized stems, salads, soups, stews, breads	Crafts, potpourri, incense	Stress, headaches, colds, coughs, indigestion, wounds, circulation, sore muscles
Anise *Pimpinella anisum*	Seeds, leaves, flowers	Breads, cakes, cookies, fruits, pickles, soups, stews, salads, curries, eggs, liqueurs	Potpourri, dog pillows	Bad breath, indigestion, coughs, colds, nausea, colic, face packs
Anise Hyssop *Agastache foeniculum*	Leaves, flowers	Fruits, cakes, cookies, teas, vegetables, grains, meats, fish	Potpourri, crafts, bouquets, attracts butterflies, cabbage moth repellent	Appetite stimulant, indigestion, nausea, chills
Arnica *Arnica montana*	Flowers			Sprains, bruises, muscle pain
Artemisia *Artemisia* species	Leaves		Moth repellent, crafts, bouquets	Hair rinse
Astragalus *Astragalus membranaceus*	Roots			Increases energy, immune resistance, circulation
Basil *Ocimum* species and cultivars	Leaves, flowers	Pestos, vinegars, salads, soups, vegetables, eggs, cheeses, meats, fish, fruits, desserts	Fly repellent, potpourri	Headaches, fevers, colds, indigestion, nausea, stress, constipation, hair rinse
Bay *Laurus nobilis*	Leaves	Soups, stews, stocks, marinades, meats, shellfish, beans, grains, custards	Crafts, potpourri, weevil repellent	Indigestion, appetite stimulant, muscle or joint pain, dandruff, skin tonic
Bergamot *Monarda didyma*	Leaves, flowers	Salads, teas, drinks, desserts, meats, sausages, jellies	Potpourri, crafts, bouquets, attracts butterflies	Colds, fevers, indigestion, nausea, insomnia, menstrual or joint pain
Black Cohosh *Cimicifuga racemosa*	Roots		Bouquets	Headaches, muscle or joint pain, menstrual problems, high blood pressure, tinnitus
Borage *Borago officinalis*	Leaves, flowers	Drinks, salads, crystallized flowers, soups, greens, dips, fish, poultry, herb blends	Bouquets, potpourri	Colds, coughs, fevers, insomnia, stress, face packs, bruises
Calendula *Calendula officinalis*	Flower petals	Salads, soups, stews, eggs, cheeses, butters, grains, desserts, drinks	Bouquets, potpourri	Skin care, indigestion, menstrual pain, mouthwash, oily hair, wounds
Caraway *Carum carvi*	Seeds, leaves	Breads, cakes, cookies, soups, sauces, meats, vegetables, cheeses, eggs, salads, desserts	Cook with cabbage to reduce odors, companion plant to peas	Appetite stimulant, indigestion, bad breath, coughs, menstrual pain
Catnip *Nepeta cataria*	Leaves	Salads, teas, stews, roasts	Cat toys, bouquets, deters insects	Colds, flu, insomnia, stress, indigestion, dandruff, bruises, joint pain, hemorrhoids
Cayenne *Capsicum annuum*	Fruit	Salsas, barbecue, soups, stews, cheeses, eggs, sauces, curries	Crafts, insect repellent	Joint or muscle pain, circulation, sore throat
Chamomile *Chamaemelum nobile*	Flowers		Cut-flower solution, potpourri, speeds compost, prevents damping off, aids plant growth	Indigestion, nausea, insomnia, hyperactivity, dandruff, skin care
Chervil *Anthriscus cerefolium*	Leaves	Salads, vegetables, chicken, fish, eggs, soups, sauces, vinegars, butters	Potpourri, bouquets, repels slugs and insects	Indigestion, liver and kidney function, skin care, joint pain, wounds

COMMON HERBS AND THEIR USES *(continued)*

Name	Parts Used	In the Kitchen	In the Home and Garden	For Health and Beauty
Chives *Allium schoenoprasum*	Leaves, flowers	Salads, vegetables, chicken, fish, eggs, cheeses, soups, sauces, vinegars, butters	Crafts, bouquets, insect and disease control	Appetite stimulant, indigestion
Cilantro, Coriander *Coriandrum sativum*	Leaves, flowers, seeds, roots	Salads, salsas, vinegars, marinades, meats, vegetables, grains, eggs, cheeses, beans	Potpourri	Appetite stimulant, indigestion, bad breath, joint pain, hemorrhoids
Comfrey *Symphytum officinale*	Leaves		Mulch, speeds compost, fertilizer	Skin care, hair rinse, wounds, bruises, sprains, joint pain, bunions, hemorrhoids
Costmary *Tanacetum balsamita*	Leaves	Salads, teas, drinks, root vegetables, game, fruitcakes	Insect repellent, rinse for linens	Colds, indigestion, cramps, hair rinse, skin care, insect bites, minor burns
Cowslip *Primula veris*	Leaves, flowers, roots	Salads, desserts, teas, crystallized flowers	Potpourri	Insomnia, stress, allergies, headaches, facial tonic, wounds, coughs, colds
Dill *Anethum graveolens*	Leaves, flowers, seeds	Salads, soups, cheeses, eggs, meats, vegetables, vinegars, pickles, herb blends, sauces	Bouquets, crafts	Indigestion, bad breath, insomnia, diuretic, coughs, colds, menstrual pain
Elder *Sambucus* species	Flowers, berries	Fritters, sorbets, teas, vinegars, wines, pies, jellies, jams	Bouquets, potpourri, attracts butterflies	Colds, coughs, eye compress, flu, arthritis, hay fever, skin care, sore throat
Elecampane *Inula helenium*	Roots, flowers	As a vegetable	Crafts, potpourri, incense, bouquets	Respiratory infections, coughs, indigestion, acne
Fennel *Foeniculum vulgare*	Leaves, seeds, flowers	Salads, soups, meats, fish, vegetables, eggs, cheeses, beans, butters, vinegars	Bouquets	Indigestion, appetite suppressant, skin care, sore throat, eye compress
Feverfew *Tanacetum parthenium*	Leaves, flowers		Potpourri, crafts, bouquets, moth repellent, disinfectant	Migraine prevention, tension, arthritis, insomnia
Garlic *Allium sativum*	Bulbs	Salads, marinades, stews, soups, beans, meats, sauces, vegetables, cheeses, vinegars	Crafts, insect and plant disease spray	Colds, flu, infections, blood pressure or cholesterol reduction, coughs, diarrhea
Ginger *Zingiber officinale*	Roots	Marinades, stir-frying, drinks, desserts, fruits, winter vegetables, crystallized roots		Colds, flu, fever, nausea, constipation, indigestion, circulation, blood pressure
Ginseng *Panax* species	Roots			Stress, nervous exhaustion, recovery from illness
Goldenseal *Hydrastis canadensis*	Roots			Stress, anxiety, indigestion, sore throat, menstrual problems, douche
Hops *Humulus lupulus*	Fruit, young shoots	Beers, as a vegetable	Crafts	Insomnia, anxiety, headaches, indigestion, menstrual pain
Horehound *Marrubium vulgare*	Leaves, flowers, seeds	Teas, drinks	Crafts, bouquets, attracts bees	Coughs, sore throat, appetite stimulant, indigestion
Horseradish *Armoracia rusticana*	Roots	Slaws, dips, beets, cream cheese, mayonnaise, sauces for roast beef or oily fish	Dispels worms in dogs, companion to potatoes, brown rot control	Coughs, stiff muscles, eliminates toxins, stimulates digestion
Horsetail *Equisetum arvense*	Stems		Bouquets, scouring metal, sanding wood	Sprains, eczema, hair rinse, fingernail strengthener
Hyssop *Hyssopus officinalis*	Leaves, flowers	Salads, soups, stews, sausages, meats, fruits, desserts, teas	Potpourri, bouquets, repels flea beetles, companion to grapes	Sore throat, respiratory infections, indigestion, wounds, bruises, skin care

COMMON HERBS AND THEIR USES *(continued)*

Name	Parts Used	In the Kitchen	In the Home and Garden	For Health and Beauty
Lady's Mantle *Alchemilla mollis*	Leaves, flowers		Bouquets, nosegays	Menstrual regulation, menopause, skin care, mouthwash, inflammations
Lavender *Lavandula* species	Leaves, flowers	Cakes, cookies, muffins, jellies, teas, vinegars, fruits, eggs, crystallized flowers	Crafts, potpourri, incense, bouquets, moth and fly repellent	Tension, headaches, bad breath, skin care, hair rinse, pain, insomnia, wounds
Lemon Balm *Melissa officinalis*	Leaves, flowers	Teas, wines, liqueurs, fish, cheese dips, fruit salads, butters, vinegars	Potpourri, furniture polish, attracts bees	Anxiety, mild depression, headaches, insomnia, indigestion, nausea, cold sores
Lemongrass *Cymbopogon citratus*	Stems, leaves	Southeast Asian dishes, stir-fries, soups, pastas, vegetables, fish, vinegars	Potpourri	Indigestion, cramps, stress, fever, joint or muscle pain
Lemon Verbena *Aloysia triphylla*	Leaves	Sauces, marinades, salad dressings, teas, drinks, vinegars, fruits, desserts	Potpourri	Massage oil, skin care, insomnia, indigestion, nausea, congestion
Licorice *Glycyrrhiza glabra*	Roots			Colds, sore throat, cramps, constipation, indigestion, arthritis, high cholesterol
Lovage *Levisticum officinale*	Leaves, stems, roots, seeds	Salads, salad dressings, soups, stocks, stews, cheeses, roast meats, pickles, sauces	Bouquets	Indigestion, diuretic, cramps, urinary tract infections, circulation, wounds
Marsh Mallow *Althaea officinalis*	Leaves, roots	Salads, as a vegetable	Attracts butterflies	Coughs, sore throats, skin care, insomnia, indigestion, dry hair, eye compress
Meadowsweet *Filipendula ulmaria*	Leaves, flowers		Bouquets, potpourri	Headaches, colds, fever, indigestion, diarrhea, insomnia, diuretic, skin care
Milk Thistle *Silybum marianum*	Leaves, flowers, roots	Salads, as a vegetable, greens	Crafts	Aids and protects liver function
Mint *Mentha* species	Leaves, flowers	Vegetables, fruits, sauces, jellies, syrups, vinegars, teas, drinks, crystallized leaves	Bouquets, potpourri, mice and insect repellent	Indigestion, colds, flu, hiccups, insomnia, skin care, oily hair
Myrtle *Myrtus communis*	Leaves, flowers, seeds	Roasts, juniper berry substitute	Potpourri, furniture polish	Urinary and vaginal infections, coughs, congestion, skin care, bruises, hemorrhoids
Oregano *Origanum vulgare*	Leaves, flowers	Salads, cheeses, eggs, tomato sauces, marinades, roasts, stews, beans, vinegars, butters	Bouquets, crafts, companion plant to beans	Indigestion, coughs, headaches, menstrual, joint, or muscle pain, seasickness
Parsley *Petroselinum crispum*	Leaves	Salads, eggs, vegetables, meats, soups, stews, roasts, vinegars, butters, sauces	Bouquets, companion plant to roses	Urinary infections, bad breath, indigestion, sprains, wounds, hair rinse, skin care
Pinks *Dianthus* species and cultivars	Flowers	Salads, fruits, desserts, vinegars, wines, jellies, sugar, crystallized flowers	Bouquets, crafts, attracts butterflies and bees	Stress, tension
Purple Coneflower *Echinacea* species	Roots, flowers		Bouquets, attracts butterflies	Colds, flu, allergies, fevers, wounds, sore throat
Rose *Rosa* species and cultivars	Flowers, fruits	Salads, teas, drinks, syrups, sugar, butters, vinegars, jams, desserts, crystallized petals	Bouquets, crafts, potpourri	Skin care, massage oil, circulation, colds, flu

COMMON HERBS AND THEIR USES *(continued)*

Name	Parts Used	In the Kitchen	In the Home and Garden	For Health and Beauty
Rosemary *Rosmarinus officinalis*	Leaves, flowers	Meats, vegetables, eggs, cheeses, breads, marinades, butters, vinegars, desserts	Potpourri, antiseptic cleaning solution	Indigestion, skin care, hair rinse, sore throat, muscle and joint pain, wounds, bruises
Rue *Ruta graveolens*	Leaves, seed pods		Crafts, insect repellent	Eye compress
Sage *Salvia officinalis*	Leaves, flowers	Vegetables, meats, eggs, cheeses, breads, fruits, butters, vinegars, jellies, teas	Crafts, insect repellent, incense, antiseptic cleaning solutions	Indigestion, diarrhea, stress, coughs, colds, menopause, skin care, sore throat
St. John's Wort *Hypericum perforatum*	Flowers			Mild depression, stress, insomnia, PMS, cold sores, shingles, burns, wounds, pain
Salad Burnet *Poterium sanguisorba*	Leaves	Salads, soups, drinks, cheeses, fish, sauces, butters, vinegars, vegetables		Diuretic, diarrhea, hemorrhoids, skin care
Savory *Satureja* species	Leaves, flowers	Beans, soups, eggs, meats, vegetables, butters, vinegars, jellies, herb blends, teas		Indigestion, sore throat, skin care, diarrhea, insect bites
Scented Geranium *Pelargonium* species and cultivars	Leaves, flowers	Desserts, jellies, butters, syrups, sugar, sorbets, vinegars, drinks	Nosegays, potpourri	Skin care
Soapwort *Saponaria officinalis*	Leaves, stems, flowers		Bouquets, soap for delicate fabrics	Soap for skin, hair, acne, eczema
Stinging Nettle *Urtica dioica*	Leaves, roots	Greens, soups, teas	Attracts butterflies, fertilizer, aphid spray, speeds composting	Hay fever, asthma, anemia, diuretic, circulation, eczema, insect bites, dandruff
Sweet Cicely *Myrrhis odorata*	Leaves, seeds, roots	Salads, fish, eggs, soups, stews, butters, vinegars, desserts, liqueurs	Furniture polish, bouquets, crafts	Coughs, anemia, indigestion
Sweet Marjoram *Origanum majorana*	Leaves, flowers	Salads, cheeses, meats, vegetables, butters, vinegars	Furniture polish, potpourri, crafts	Colds, coughs, sore throat, headaches, insomnia, muscle or joint pain, hair rinse
Sweet Woodruff *Galium odoratum*	Leaves	Wines	Potpourri, insect repellent, crafts	
Tansy *Tanacetum vulgare*	Leaves, flowers		Bouquets, crafts, insect repellent, enriches compost	
Tarragon *Artemisia dracunculus*	Leaves	Salads, eggs, sauces, soups, grains, fish, poultry, cheeses, vinegars, butters, liqueurs	Enhances growth of vegetables	Health tonic, appetite stimulant, indigestion
Thyme *Thymus* species and cultivar	Leaves, flowers	Salads, stews, soups, sauces, meats, eggs, vegetables, cheeses, grains, vinegars	Nosegays, disinfectant, potpourri, insect repellent, companion plant	Indigestion, congestion, skin care, insomnia, hangovers, dandruff, sore throat, wounds
Valerian *Valeriana officinalis*	Roots		Improves compost, attracts earthworms, boosts vegetable growth, cat pillows	Insomnia, anxiety, tension, high blood pressure, skin care
Viola, Violet, Heartsease *Viola* species and cultivars	Leaves, flowers	Salads, desserts, drinks, syrups, jellies, vinegars, butters, crystallized flowers	Bouquets, nosegays, potpourri, crafts	Colds, coughs, congestion, arthritis, cystitis, skin care, hair rinse
Yarrow *Achillea* species and cultivars	Leaves, flowers	Salads, butters, cheeses	Bouquets, crafts, attracts beneficial insects, speeds composting	Colds, flu, arthritis, blood pressure, circulation, wounds, menstrual problems, skin care

GROWING AND PRESERVING

When preparing an herb garden, remove existing vegetation, spread at least a 3- to 6-inch layer of organic matter on top of the soil, sprinkle on dry fertilizer. Add lime and other amendments according to soil-test recommendations, then mix everything into the soil at least 8 to 12 inches deep.

Even though many herbs adapt to a range of soils and climates, you can achieve the greatest gardening success by matching the plants you choose to your site's growing conditions.

First, select woody and perennial herbs that thrive in your climate. They need to be able to survive the minimum temperature expected in your area, delineated by the U.S.D.A. Plant Hardiness Zone Map of North America (see page 93).

They also must be able to handle your area's summer heat and humidity. The understanding of plants' heat hardiness is still in its infancy, so talk with other gardeners in your area to find out which herbs do best in your region. One way to successfully grow plants that may be adversely affected by heat and humidity is to plant them in a location that is lightly shaded in the afternoon. However, in very warm areas, this won't help herbs that are extremely sensitive to heat and humidity.

You also should keep in mind the amount of sunlight in different parts of your yard, your garden's soil type and drainage patterns, and typical rainfall in your area. All these factors influence where, how, and what you grow.

Next, consider the average times of the first and last frost dates in your area so that you can plant, prune, and harvest accordingly. Be aware, too, of the wind in your garden, which can affect winter hardiness as well as moisture loss from plants.

PREPARING SOIL

Soil anchors plants and is the source of nutrients and water. Because soil is so important, an herb garden should have the best soil possible. If your soil needs improvement, it will be much easier to do before planting.

Start by testing the soil for nutrient levels, especially nitrogen, phosphorus, and potassium. County extension offices and professional laboratories (check the Yellow Pages) do the tests. Or you can buy a soil-test kit, available at garden centers or from mail-order sources, to test the soil yourself.

Both the extension office and private labs will provide guidelines for correcting deficiencies. With home tests, as a general rule, if nitrogen is in the average or moderate range, spread a 3-inch layer of compost over the area and work it into the soil. If nitrogen levels are low, make the layer 6 inches deep.

If phosphorus is low, apply 30 to 50 pounds of rock phosphate per 1,000 square feet. For low potassium, apply 50 to 100 pounds of greensand (a potassium-containing sediment mixed with clay or sand) per 1,000 square feet. For average phosphorous or potassium levels, use half as much of these minerals. These rates will supply enough phosphorus and potassium to keep herbs healthy for four or five years.

At the same time as you test soil nutrients, test for pH levels, which affect nutrient availability. The pH of a soil refers to its degree of acidity or alkalinity. A pH of 7 is neutral. Lower numbers indicate acidity, higher numbers, alkalinity. Most herbs do best with a pH range of 6 to 7. Use agricultural limestone to raise pH and ground elemental sulfur to lower it.

Adequate soil drainage is important for many herbs, which is why herbs are often grown in raised beds like these. To determine the drainage of your soil, dig a hole 12 inches deep and fill with water. If the water is gone in 30 minutes, your drainage is adequate.

Whatever the soil's type (sand, clay or loam), add organic matter to aid water absorption, improve drainage and aeration, make soil easier to work, and easier for roots to grow in. It's best to prepare the soil for your herb bed well ahead of time. For spring planting, prepare the bed the fall before. For fall planting, start in spring.

Spread a 3-inch layer of compost on dry soil with the rock phosphate, greensand, and lime or sulfur called for. Then, thoroughly dig all these materials into the soil. Be sure not to work clay soil when it is wet, or you'll end up with hard, bricklike clumps. After tilling or digging, rake the area smooth. Now you're ready to plant the best herb garden ever!

Winter protection, such as providing windbreaks or covering plants loosely with pine boughs or leaves, is important if your area does not get much snow for insulation or if you are trying to grow plants that are marginally hardy.

Light is key to growing herbs. Most herbs do best with at least six hours of sunlight each day. If you have a shady yard, grow herbs that can tolerate less light, or remove some of the trees.

GETTING STARTED

Buying herb plants in the spring from a reputable herb nursery or garden center is the quickest and easiest way to get your herb garden started.

You can easily start an herb garden by buying seedlings at a garden center or starting them from seed at home, either planting the seeds directly into the garden or germinating them indoors. Many herbs are not that difficult to start from seed.

BUYING

Buying herbs as seedlings, rather than starting them yourself from seed, saves time, money, and the effort involved in raising transplants, especially if you want just one or two plants of each herb. Also, some, like French tarragon or named cultivars of other herbs, either do not produce seed or do not come true to form from seed and can be propagated only from cuttings or by division.

Not long ago, herb plants were difficult to find. Now, the most common herbs are readily available in spring at discount department stores, hardware stores, and garden centers.

When looking for some of the more unusual herbs, among the best sources are specialized herb nurseries, local herb society plant sales, and mail-order sources. If you are unfamiliar with a mail-order company, it is best to make your first order small. Open boxes of mail-ordered plants immediately, water them well, and place the plants in indirect light, then move them to the garden or repot them within the next several days.

STARTING SEEDS

OUTDOORS: The best herbs to sow directly into the garden are the ones that germinate quickly and easily, that you want in quantity, or that do not transplant well. Basil, chervil, cilantro, fennel, and dill are among the herbs to consider sowing directly.

Just as with vegetables, it is best to plant certain herbs in early spring because they are cool-season plants. These include dill, chervil, and coriander (also called cilantro). Do not plant the more tender ones until the danger of frost is past. Warm-season plants include basil and fennel. Check the individual herbs in the encyclopedia starting on page 56 or check seed packets for recommended outdoor planting times for each herb.

Before planting seeds outdoors, prepare a weed-free, smooth seedbed of crumbly soil, enriched with organic matter and fertilizer. Mark rows with a string line, as you would when planting vegetables. Using a hoe or the tip of a trowel, dig a shallow depression in the soil along the string. How deep to make the depression depends on the specific herb's ideal planting depth. Sow the seeds in the bottom of the depression, lightly cover them with a thin layer of soil, and gently tamp the soil with the tines of a garden rake.

Label the row with the name of the herb and the planting date. Gently water the area and keep it moist until seedlings appear. When the seedlings are 1 to 2 inches tall, thin the plants to about 4 inches apart. Thin by snipping the unwanted plants off at ground level with scissors to avoid disturbing the roots of the remaining plants.

INDOORS: Successfully starting your own herbs from seeds indoors can be a challenging but rewarding experience. Start perennial herbs 10 to 12 weeks before the last frost date for your area because they can be slower to germinate and to reach transplanting size than annual herbs, which are best sown 6 to 8 weeks before the last frost is expected.

First, select a container to hold the seed-starting mix. Among the simplest and least expensive is a plastic tray-and-dome set. These are available at hardware, drug, discount department, and garden supply stores. With care, you can reuse one for several years; before reusing, wash it thoroughly with soapy water mixed with a little ammonia or disinfectant.

Next, purchase a sterile seed-starting mix, which usually is sold where you bought the tray. Using a clean container and sterile soil mix prevents seedlings that are started indoors from dying of a disease called "damping off," which rots seedlings at the soil line.

Before sowing the seeds, pour warm water into the bag of seed-starting mix. With your hands, stir the mix, adding more water, if necessary, until the mix is thoroughly moistened. If the bag doesn't have enough room for you to work without spilling, put the soil mix into a bucket or other container. After moistening the soil, pour it into the seed-starting container and plant the seeds.

To keep the seed-starting medium and the atmosphere around germinating seeds moist, loosely cover the tray with a piece of glass, plastic, or the clear dome that came with the tray.

Most seeds need a soil temperature of about 75° F to germinate. To achieve this temperature, some people simply set their seed trays on top of the refrigerator or a heat register. There are also heating mats designed for this purpose. After the seeds have sprouted, remove them from the heat source.

Seedlings require temperatures of 60° to 70° F and bright light to grow well. If you do not have a window that gets lots of sunlight, consider buying a fluorescent light unit. The ones that hold four tubes are best. Outfit it with either special grow-light bulbs or two each of warm-white and cool-white fluorescent tubes. If desired, attach the cord to a timer. Set the timer so the lights are left on 14 to 16 hours each day.

When the seedlings are 1 to 2 inches tall and have developed true leaves—the second pair of leaves to develop after germination—transplant the herbs to individual 2- to 4-inch pots.

Continue growing them in pots under lights, watering and fertilizing them regularly, according to the manufacturer's directions, until about a week before they are to be transplanted into the garden.

Then, harden off the plants by taking them outdoors and setting them in a sheltered spot. If frost is expected, cover them or temporarily bring them back indoors.

PLANTING

Moving plants to the garden can be stressful for the plants. To ease the transition, water the potted plants thoroughly just before transplanting.

Transplant when the soil is moderately dry and crumbly and when the weather is cloudy just before a rain. If the weather is hot and dry, transplant at dusk. If the herb is frost-sensitive, wait to transplant it until all danger of frost is past. Set out the hardier herbs, especially the perennials and the cool-season annuals, several weeks before your area's last expected frost.

To plant, position the seedling in the hole so that it is at the same depth as it was in the container. Fill in around the roots with soil. Tamp gently with your fingers, then add more soil if necessary.

Label, and then water the new plant with a soaker hose or sprinkling can. Some gardeners water-in new plantings using special fertilizers developed to help transplanted seedlings quickly develop new roots and to lessen transplant shock.

1. Grasp the herb stem at the soil level and carefully pull it from the pot. If it does not come out easily, hold it upside down and sharply tap the edge of the pot. If roots are massed tightly, gently loosen them with your fingers.

2. Dig the planting hole as deep as the herb's rootball and two to three times wider. This loosens the soil, making it easier for roots to spread out. Set the plant in the hole at the same depth as it grew in the pot.

CARE

To have healthy herbs that provide an abundance of leaves or flowers for cooking, health, and fragrance, you must take care of them. That means watering, weeding, fertilizing, mulching, controlling pests, and providing protection for herbs in winter.

WATERING

Most herbs are adaptable plants and thrive in a range of moisture conditions. They'll tolerate nearly anything except being too wet. By mixing organic matter into the soil, you will ensure a well-drained planting area that supplies adequate water to plants.

If you're growing a variety of herbs, it's wise to learn about each one to know how much water each needs. Take into account the herb's native habitat, which will indicate whether the plant has adapted to dry or wet conditions, and whether it has deep or shallow roots. Then consider the effect of environmental factors on your plants, such as rainfall, wind, day and night temperatures, and soil drainage.

A plant with shallow roots will need more frequent watering than one with an extensive, deep root system. High temperatures, brisk winds, and fast-draining soil also increase the amount of water you need to apply.

The best way to determine when to water is to periodically check plants and soil. As plants become drought-stressed, leaves turn a dull color, then wilt. Assess soil moisture by digging down several inches; if more than the surface inch or so is dry, water probably is needed.

The best time to water is early in the morning. Use a soaker hose or a hose fitted with a water-breaker nozzle, available at garden centers. Water slowly and deeply to prevent runoff and to encourage deep roots that are better able to survive drought.

WEEDING

Weeds compete with other plants for water, light, and nutrients. Frequently check your garden and remove weeds when they are small. By keeping on top of things, weeds have no chance to crowd their neighbors or to disturb the roots of nearby herbs when you pull them. Although weeding can be a lot of work, look on it as an opportunity to get close to your herbs and enjoy their fragrance.

Make sure you're familiar with the appearance of your herbs, especially perennial species, so you remove only weeds and not herbs, too. If weeds grow large enough to take a clump of soil with them as you pull them, refill the space with compost or topsoil. To

Remove weeds when they are small so they don't overgrow your herbs. Gently hold the herb stem, then carefully pull the weed out.

minimize weeding, spread several inches of mulch over the herb bed.

FERTILIZING

Herbs, like other plants, manufacture food through photosynthesis, using the energy of the sun to turn water and air into starches. The soil supplies other raw materials—minerals dissolved in the water that plants absorb from the soil—to carry on this and other life processes. If your soil does not have enough of these nutrient minerals, you must supply them.

The nutrients plants need in the greatest quantity are nitrogen, phosphorus, and potassium. But herbs receiving high levels of nutrients, particularly nitrogen, produce inferior growth with little flavor or fragrance. For that reason, try to keep your garden's soil fertility level in the average-to-fertile range.

In midsummer, lightly scratch a tablespoon of fertilizer into the soil around the roots of lush, fast-growing herbs such as basil.

To do this, build up the soil with compost or other organic matter, rock phosphate, and greensand before planting, as described on page 13. Mix in fertilizer following soil test recommendations. This is all the fertilizer required the first year. In following years, you may find that applying an organic mulch annually provides enough nutrients for herbs. Test your soil each spring to determine whether this is so or if additional nutrients are needed to stay in the average-to-fertile range.

Many types and formulations of fertilizers are available, including ones that you apply dry and lightly work into the soil and others that you dissolve in water and spray on plants. Of these, the easiest to use are the complete granular fertilizers, which contain the three major nutrients, represented by numbers such

Mulching is good, but taper the mulch layer near the base of plants to avoid disease.

as 3-6-3. Apply these in spring at the rate suggested by a soil test or follow the manufacturer's directions on the label. Some products contain a controlled-release form of nitrogen, such as methylene urea, which produces the slow, steady growth that is best for herbs. Organic fertilizers, made from plant, animal, or natural mineral sources, also release nutrients slowly, and they slightly increase the humus in the soil.

Individual herbs have specific nutrient needs. Check the encyclopedia starting on page 56 for individual recommendations.

MULCHING

A 2-inch layer of organic mulch, such as compost, pulverized bark, or cocoa hulls inhibits weeds, moderates soil moisture and temperature, prevents erosion, increases soil

fertility and tilth, and keeps plants clean.

Apply a new layer of mulch every spring, after the soil has warmed. Before mulching, remove weeds from your site and scratch the soil surface lightly with a hoe or hand cultivator to break the crust. Taper the mulch layer near the base of plants where it could hold moisture and rot stems.

PEST CONTROL

With adequate soil fertility and water, herbs generally have few pest problems. But at times, they can fall victim to the same pests that are the bane of all gardeners: aphids, whiteflies, caterpillars, and slugs. Bay, in particular, is singled out by scale insects.

To control these insects, encourage natural predators, such as birds, bats, toads, and ladybugs, or use simple controls such as slug traps or sticky traps. If these methods fail, apply a food-safe insecticide, such as pyrethrin, *Bacillus thuringiensis* (Bt) or insecticidal soap. Spray in the evening when beneficial insects have stopped flying. As for insects such as the larvae of the swallowtail butterfly—which feast on parsley, dill, and fennel foliage—grow enough plants to supply both you and them. Indoors, choose food-safe controls formulated for indoor application.

Fungal diseases are more difficult to control, so practice preventive measures of good soil drainage and air circulation.

WINTER PROTECTION

Herbs that are reliably hardy in your area can succumb to cold if planted in a windy area or in soil with poor drainage. Plan ahead by establishing windbreaks and ensuring good drainage. Alternate periods of freezing and thawing can push plants out of the ground in areas with cold temperatures but little snow. Leaving the spent foliage and stems on perennial herbs helps to protect plants in winter. A more attractive alternative is to cut back plants and mulch them loosely with pine boughs or oak leaves. Don't use leaves that mat down, such as those of maples.

Be sure to remove any tree leaves that fall on evergreen or prostrate plants like the thymes. Leaving them could rot the plants.

HOMEMADE PEST CONTROLS

Among the safe methods of controlling insect pests are two homemade pest controls. You may want to get an inexpensive blender just for this purpose, as the "bug juice" method requires collecting about ½ cup of the insect pests and blending them with 2 cups of water. After liquefying, strain and dilute ¼ cup of the pureed insects with 1 gallon of water in a hand sprayer. Freeze the remainder, marking it clearly.

Another spray is made by pureeing ¼ cup hot pepper, ¼ cup garlic cloves and 2 cups of water in a blender. Strain and dilute in the same way as the bug juice.

PRUNING

runing shapes herbs and helps them produce plenty of flavorful growth to harvest. The correct pruning times and methods vary from herb to herb, so check the encyclopedia starting on page 56 for specific information. Always use a sharp pair of garden scissors or pruners when pruning or harvesting because stems damaged by dull tools are susceptible to disease.

In general, prune shrubby perennial herbs with woody stems, such as sage or rosemary, in spring, removing dead branches and cutting the rest of the stems back by half. This keeps the plants bushy and well shaped. Trim several inches of the stems in midsummer to initiate fresh, tender growth during the latter half of the gardening season. Do not prune woody perennial herbs later than eight weeks

Prune herbs regularly to maintain their shape and size. This also initiates additional growth.

before the first frost. If these plants are pruned too late in the season, the new growth will not have enough time to harden before freezing weather arrives.

CREATING A STANDARD

Standards result from a highly formalized pruning style that trains a woody plant to a single, straight, bare stem topped with a round- or cone-shaped head of leaves.

These plants are often grown in containers outdoors, where they serve as a stunning focal point, then are overwintered indoors. The best plants to use for a standard include bay, rosemary, lavender, santolina, helichrysum, myrtle, and small-leaved scented geraniums.

Before starting a standard, decide on its ultimate size, keeping the proportions of the container, stem, and head in balance. Choose a rooted cutting or young plant with a single stem. Insert a stake next to the stem and loosely tie the cutting to it.

When the plant is about 6 inches shorter than the desired finished height, pinch off its growing tip (left photo, below). Cut side shoots below the desired bottom of the head back to the main stem to bare the stem between the soil and the head. Finally, trim each side shoot in the head area so that only two to three leaves or sets of leaves remain. When these side shoots have formed four or five new leaves or leaf sets, again trim them back to two or three leaves or leaf sets. Repeat this step until the head is full, shaped the way you want it and at its final height.

To maintain the standard, prune it in spring and late summer and whenever growth requires reshaping.

PROPAGATION

Multiplying herbs by cuttings, layering, or division is easy and inexpensive. It also provides you with an opportunity to share favorite plants with friends.

Rooting cuttings taken from the stems of woody herbs is a simple way to get many new plants. There are three main types of woody stem cuttings:

SOFTWOOD CUTTINGS: Spring and early-summer cuttings from new growth that has not yet hardened.

SEMI-HARDWOOD CUTTINGS: Midsummer cuttings from growth that has started to harden at the base.

HARDWOOD CUTTINGS: Late-season cuttings made from fully hardened wood.

For all three types, cut 4- to 6-inch-long sturdy pieces of stem, making the cut just above a leaf. Next, pinch off the lower third of the leaves, taking care to not tear the stem. Dust or dip the stripped end in a powder or liquid rooting hormone.

Carefully remove leaves from the lower third of the cutting, the portion inserted into the rooting medium. Leaves left on the cutting could rot.

With a pencil or chopstick, make a hole in a pot of moistened, sterile potting soil, horticultural vermiculite, or perlite. Insert the stem up to the bottom of the leaves and firm the potting medium around it. Add more cuttings to the pot, about 2 inches apart. Insert a label with the name of the plant and the date. Cover the pot with a plastic dome or bag, making sure it does not touch the leaves. The dome holds in moisture and keeps cuttings from wilting, but it also can cook plants by holding in heat. Keep the pot out of direct sunlight and open the dome a crack to let heat escape.

Set the pot in a spot with bright, indirect light and keep the medium moist. Placing the pot on a heating mat speeds rooting. When cuttings show signs of growth, usually after four to six weeks, remove the dome. When you tug on the cutting and it resists being pulled out of the pot, it is developing roots. How long that takes varies with the species of herb. At this point, pot up the plant and move it to the garden.

Many herbs, including mint, basil, rosemary, oregano, and thyme, will root in water if they are not too woody.

LAYERING

Layering is a good way to propagate low-growing or creeping plants that are difficult to root from cuttings. With layering, rooting occurs while the stem is still attached to the plant.

Bend a shoot to the ground. Scoop out a small hole in the soil where the shoot touches the ground, then hold the stem in place with an old-fashioned, peg-type clothespin or a hairpin-shaped piece of wire. Cover the pegged section with soil and gently firm.

Keep the area moist until new growth develops; then cut the newly rooted plant from the main plant and transplant it immediately.

To maintain humidity levels, loosely cover the pot with plastic.

DIVIDING

Many perennial herbs, such as oregano and lemon balm, send out an ever-widening circle of growth. These new plants crowd the original plant, which then declines. Dig up an overgrown clump and cut or break it apart. Depending on the plant, an alternative is to dig small plants at the edge of the clump. Early spring or fall are the best times to divide.

To speed rooting when layering, make a small nick in the portion of stem that is placed in the soil. Use this method with thicker-stemmed plants like sage or rosemary.

To divide a large, thickly rooted plant clump, put two spading forks back to back in the center and pry the roots apart.

When layering, hold the bent stem securely in the ground with a hairpin-shaped piece of wire or a peg-type clothespin.

GROWING HERBS INDOORS

The idyllic vision of pots of fresh herbs thriving on a windowsill while bitter winds blow and snow piles up outside is hard to resist. Unfortunately, you'll find reality is somewhat removed from this fantasy. Most houseplants are from the tropics, while the majority of herbs are woody plants from temperate climates and do not adjust well to the indoor environment.

Still, if you can provide enough light, space, and other conditions, a number of herbs can be grown indoors, either during the winter or throughout the year.

LIGHT

The most important condition for growing herbs indoors is bright light. If you can successfully grow flowering houseplants, your windowsill probably has enough natural light for herbs. When growing plants on a windowsill, turn pots regularly so that all sides receive light.

If you can't provide enough sunlight, an alternative is to use a fluorescent lighting unit, preferably one with four tubes. Outfit this either with grow lights or with an equal number of warm- and cool-white fluorescent tubes.

Another possibility is to use a metal halide light unit. These are available from mail-order companies that specialize in hydroponic units (ebb-and-flow water-culture units). They are easy to set up and require no special wiring.

Leave supplemental lighting on for 12 to 14 hours each day. Use an inexpensive automatic timer to turn lights off and on.

To successfully grow herbs indoors, you'll need bright light, cool to moderate temperatures, and adequate humidity. The way to start is to pot young transplants in late summer or fall, or sow seeds directly into a container.

TEMPERATURE, HUMIDITY, AND AIR MOVEMENT

Temperature, humidity, and air movement are other conditions to take into consideration when growing herbs indoors. Most herbs, especially the ones from temperate climates, do their best with indoor temperatures that are 60° to 70° F during the day and at least 10° cooler at night.

Because air in homes is much drier than in most outdoor environments, it's necessary to raise the humidity around plants. This is accomplished in several ways, including grouping plants together or setting them on trays of gravel, sand, or capillary matting. Spider mites on plants indoors are a sure sign that humidity is too low, while fungal diseases indicate that humidity is too high.

Keep moist air moving gently around plants to help prevent fungal disease. Placing a small fan near the plants is simple and effective.

SOIL, WATER, AND FERTILIZER

Although some people dig up herbs from the garden in the fall and put them into pots, you'll have the best success growing herbs indoors by either bringing in herbs that have been growing in pots all summer or by planting seeds or young plants directly into pots. Use a commercial potting soil or mix your own from equal parts topsoil, perlite, peat moss or composted bark, and coarse sand.

Water herbs regularly, letting the soil dry slightly between waterings. Use a water-soluble houseplant fertilizer following the package directions or mix a slow-release fertilizer into the soil before planting.

SUGGESTED HERBS FOR INDOORS

Among the best herbs to grow indoors are the various thymes, parsley, chives, marjoram, oregano, rosemary, and shorter types of basil. Start dill, cilantro, chervil, or fennel from seed and use the plants when small.

Don't limit yourself to following just these suggestions, however. If you have a favorite herb that would bring you pleasure indoors, by all means try growing it. And if your herbs don't survive the entire winter on your windowsill, at least you can enjoy whatever amount of time they do survive. They've given you pleasure as cold winds blow outdoors.

TROPICAL HERBS

The staples of the culinary herb world have expanded dramatically in recent years. With increasing interest in Asian, Caribbean, and South American cooking, once-rare tropical herbs are becoming available in grocery produce departments and from mail-order and local herb nurseries. Almost all of these herbs are tender plants that do not withstand freezing. They are best grown in pots, summered outdoors, then brought indoors during winter. They need bright light and slightly warmer temperatures indoors than temperate-climate herbs.

■ **Cuban oregano** (*Plectranthus amboinicus*) is originally from Southeast Asia but has been widely adopted in the Caribbean and Mexico. It has a flavor that combines that of oregano with thyme and savory. Plants form spreading mounds 2 to 3 feet wide and as tall, with fleshy, velvety, oval leaves up to 2 inches long. Hardy to zone 9, Cuban oregano is best grown in full sun in a sandy, quick-draining potting soil. Pinch back growing tips to maintain the plant's bushy appearance. Propagate plants from stem cuttings taken in late summer.

■ **Curry leaf** (*Murraya koenigii*) is not to be confused with the fragrant but nonculinary curry plant (*Helichrysum italicum*). Curry leaf is a small evergreen tree, native to India, Pakistan, and Sri Lanka. Its fresh leaves are used in curry dishes. Plants grow to 20 feet tall in the tropics; but in containers in temperate climates, it reaches about 5 feet. Long, drooping, palmlike leaves are composed of narrow, 2-inch-long, shiny green leaflets. Sprays of white flowers are followed by black berries. Hardy to zone 9, it grows in full sun to light shade and in standard potting soil. Trim plants to encourage bushy growth. Curry leaf is difficult to grow from seed but can be propagated by cutting off sucker plants at the base of the mother plant.

■ **Ginger** (*Zingiber officinale*) is a perennial native to tropical Asia with reedlike stems and long, narrow leaves. Its fleshy rhizome, with its sweet-pungent flavor, has been used for culinary and medicinal purposes since earliest times. The related Japanese ginger (*Zingiber mioga*) has a bergamot-like flavor. Both are hardy to zone 10. Plant roots shallowly on their side in early spring in pots with standard potting soil. With enough warmth and light for 10 months before they go dormant, gingers will produce a good quantity of new rhizomes. Keep the soil evenly moist when plants are actively growing. Let it dry out between waterings when plants are dormant. Propagate ginger by division in late spring as growth resumes.

■ **Galangal** is the common name for a number of related tropical perennial herbs. Among the most widely used is the greater galangal (*Alpinia galanga*), also known as Thai or Siamese ginger or laos. It resembles ginger in appearance and flavor. The fresh rhizome is popular in Indonesian and Malaysian food, where the flowers and young shoots are also eaten. Two different plants are commonly called lesser galangal. The rhizome of *Alpinia officinarum* has been a medicinal herb as well as a flavoring since ancient times in China. The other lesser galangal (*Kaempferia galanga*), also known as resurrection

lily, has fingerlike tubers with yellow-orange interiors. Hardy to zone 8, the galangals are planted and grown like ginger, but they are not as apt to go dormant, and they take longer to develop rhizomes.

■ **Kaffir lime** (*Citrus hystrix*) is a small, shrubby tree, with lemon-scented leaves for flavoring curries, fish, soup, and other Southeast Asian foods. The rind and juice of the knobby fruit are also used in cooking, and the leaves, fruit, juice, and bark have medicinal uses. Leaves are unusual: leathery, shiny green, and pointed with a deep indentation in the middle that makes each half look like a separate leaf. Grow Kaffir lime in pots in standard potting soil and full sun. It is hardy to zone 10. During winter, let the top half inch of the soil dry before watering. If leaves start to yellow, fertilize with an iron-chelate containing fertilizer. Propagate Kaffir lime from cuttings.

■ **Lemongrass** (*Cymbopogon citratus*), native to southern India and Sri Lanka, forms large, to 2 foot, clumps of grassy, lemon-scented leaves. The fleshy base of the plant and its leaves flavor foods, while the leaves make a relaxing tea. Related plants are the source of citronella oil. Lemongrass is hardy to zone 9. Grow it in standard potting soil and full sun. Keep soil evenly moist. Propagate plants by division.

Lemongrass

■ **Roselle** (*Hibiscus sabdariffa*), also known as Jamaica, Indian, or Guinea sorrel as well as Florida cranberry, is a woody shrub. Some varieties have lobed, rhubarb-flavored leaves. Behind the pale yellow flowers are vitamin-C-rich, red calyces (small leaves at the base of the flower). These color and flavor herb teas and are made into jams, chutneys, or sauces. Hardy to zone 8, roselle grows in standard potting soil and full sun. Propagate it from seeds or cuttings.

■ **Turmeric** (*Curcuma longa*) is a 3-foot perennial native of India with long, broad leaves. For centuries, the pungent rhizomes have flavored foods and served as medicine. The easily recognized bright yellow-orange color of the dried and powdered rhizome is readily identifiable in curry powder and the robes of Buddhist monks. Plant and grow turmeric like ginger. Plants are dormant in winter.

HARVESTING AND PRESERVING HERBS

Harvesting herbs is one of the most pleasurable aspects of growing them. When using herbs fresh, simply cut what you need when you need it. This serves to keep plants lightly pruned. But if you are harvesting to preserve herbs, do it in ways that maximize the herbs' essential oils. The timing and method depends on the part of the plant you harvest. Gather only as much as you can process at one time, and keep herbs separate and clearly labeled.

HARVESTING FOR PRESERVING

LEAVES: The concentration of essential oils in leaves is highest just before flowers begin to develop. The best time to collect leaves is in the morning, after the dew has dried and before the day warms up. Cut stems or leaves with sharp scissors or pruning shears, then lay them gently in a gathering basket.

FLOWERS: Gather just-opening flowers at midday. For flowers on stalks, such as lavender, snip off the entire stem. When preserving individual flowers, pick each one separately. Avoid touching petals and do not harvest damaged or wilted flowers. Gently place each flower in a gathering basket.

SEEDS: Harvest seeds on a warm day when they are fully ripe but haven't begun to fall. Usually, this is when all the seeds are hard and pods are paper-dry, colored beige, brown, or black with no green showing. Cut seed heads from herbs such as dill, coriander, chervil, and fennel directly into a box or paper bag.

ROOTS: Dig up roots in fall when tops begin to die. Roots of annuals are ready to harvest the first year after planting. Perennial roots take several years to reach full growth. Carefully dig the entire plant. Cut off and compost the tops. If desired, save a few clumps of perennials for replanting.

AIR DRYING

There are several ways to air-dry leaves, including hanging them, spreading them on a screen drying rack, or using a dehydrator. When drying herbs, the work area always should be dark, dry, warm, and well ventilated.

LEAVES AND FLOWERS: Discard old or damaged flowers or leaves. If soil has splashed on them, rinse it off in cool water, then let the herbs dry. Otherwise, do not wash them.

Strip leaves of large-leaved herbs, such as basil and mint, from the stem. Spread them on the drying screen in a single layer. Cover

The simplest way to dry herbs is to gather small bunches together and hang them. Put seed heads in paper bags to catch the seeds.

basil with a sheet of newspaper to preserve its color.

To dry herbs by hanging, gather small bunches together, securing their ends with a rubber band, then hang the bunches upside down. If you use a dehydrator, follow the manufacturer's directions. Stripping leaves from stems will speed the process.

Herbs are dry when the leaves or flowers are brittle like cornflakes. If herbs have been dried on stems, gently strip off leaves on dry paper before storing. With some herbs, especially lavender, you may want to leave the flowers on the stems.

Dry sliced roots on a baking sheet at the lowest oven setting.

SEEDS: Gather several stems of seed heads into a bunch and tie them loosely together. Hang the bunches over a box or paper bag with the seed head facing down. Or, cover seed heads with a piece of muslin or cheesecloth. When they are completely dry and the seeds are falling out, gently rub the seed heads to remove any remaining seeds. Remove any nonseed plant parts by either shaking the seeds in a fine sieve or gently blowing off the debris.

ROOTS: Carefully wash the soil off the roots. For plants with taproots and thick skin, such as comfrey, licorice, and marsh mallow, scrub and peel the roots. Cut the roots into ⅛-inch-thick slices or small pieces, using a sharp knife. Spread the pieces on a cookie sheet lined with baking parchment paper. Dry them in an oven at the lowest setting. Cool completely before storing.

MICROWAVE DRYING

Drying decorative herbs and flowers in a microwave oven is fast but also problematic due to the variations in oven wattage and the type, quantity, and moisture content of the herb.

Spread herbs in a single layer on a paper towel, then cover them with another towel. Cook them on high for 30 seconds. Check their progress; then repeat until the herbs are crisp. This method is not recommended for culinary herbs. Culinary herbs release their essential oils at between 85° and 110° F. Microwaved leaves are colorful but have little flavor.

For herbs that lose their flavor when dried, freezing is an effective method of preservation. Either put clean, dry leaves in a plastic freezer bag or puree them and freeze as cubes.

FREEZING

Freezing is a particularly effective method for preserving herbs that lose their flavor when dried and for herbs with soft leaves. Among the herbs you should consider preserving by freezing are chives, chervil, tarragon, basil, parsley, dill, fennel, salad burnet, sweet cicely, and mint.

To freeze herbs, put clean, dry individual leaves or sprigs into plastic freezer bags, seal the bags, and label them. Double-bagging will reduce dehydration and preserve the herbs' flavor better. If freezing a lot of herbs, put them all together in a larger container to make organization easier.

Another method of freezing herbs is to puree herbs in a blender with a small amount of water. Then pour the slurry into ice cube trays and freeze it. After they are solid, remove the herbal ice cubes and transfer them to labeled plastic freezer bags. You can add a cube or two to a dish to give an almost-fresh flavor.

STORING DRIED HERBS

First and foremost when storing dried herbs, make sure they are totally dry, otherwise they will mold in the jars and then will be unusable. A good rule of thumb is to check jars for condensation after about a week. If you immediately attend to moisture, sometimes you can salvage part of the contents by redrying the herbs.

Glass jars, preferably dark-colored ones, are best for storing dried herbs. Although more herbs can be stored in a smaller space by crushing them, some flavor will be lost if you do this. It's best to leave herbs whole and pack jars loosely.

Cover the jars with tight-fitting lids. It's important to keep air out of the jars. Label each jar with the name of the herb and date. Store them in a dark pantry or closet.

Dried herbs lose much of their flavor or active constituents after a year. Use older herbs in potpourris or add them to the compost pile.

When the herbs are dry, loosely pack them in dark-colored glass jars with tight-fitting lids. Label each jar with the name of the herb and the date. Store them in a dark pantry.

DESIGNING WITH HERBS

Let your imagination fly when planning your herb garden. And don't be intimidated by this stage. Draw on ideas from photos and memories of herb gardens for inspiration. And remember, there is no right or wrong in design.

Because of their beauty and usefulness, as well as their range of sizes, shapes, colors, and textures, herbs offer a limitless palette for the landscape. They fit readily into flower and shrub borders, foundation plantings, vegetable gardens, and container plantings, as well as make an enchanting garden all by themselves.

PLANNING

Certainly, some people can go to the garden center, bring home a bunch of plants, and create a spectacular garden. But the rest of us will be much more successful if we develop at least a rudimentary plan before going shopping.

First, walk around your yard to decide where to locate the bed. Think about where you would like to use herbs in the garden and how accessible the herb garden needs to be. Planting close to the house makes it easy to run to the garden for a sprig of something as you cook. But you might enjoy having the

garden in a secluded location where you go to meditate. Of course, don't forget to check a potential site's growing conditions.

As you choose the site, consider how the bed will appear from your main vantage point. Not only do you want to choose a site that offers the most satisfactory view, but it should also be able to accommodate the size and shape of bed you are planning.

PLOTTING

Once you've chosen a site for the garden, measure it. Include areas adjacent to the bed that will be part of the garden's background because for the herb garden to blend seamlessly into your landscape, you need to consider the entire area as part of the design.

After measuring, you're ready to do some plotting on paper. Don't be intimidated by this stage. Gather notepads, graph paper, tracing paper, pencils, ruler, and most importantly, erasers. Draw the area to scale on

Exciting color combinations abound when you contrast purple-leaved herbs with yellow- or variegated-leaved herbs.

Although this cottage-style herb garden has a casual feel, its pulled-together look results from careful planning. The use of yellow-flowered herbs throughout the garden creates unity.

Formal garden designs are based on symmetrical balance, with each half the mirror image of the other.

Garden structures are best built from materials that complement the style and materials of your home and surrounding landscape. Here, weathered wood shows up in the garage, the neighbor's fence, and the pickets.

graph paper. An architect's scale available at art supply stores helps you plot the "inches." Then, mark in any permanent fixtures.

Now lay a sheet of tracing paper over the scale drawing and begin experimenting with overall garden plans. Use separate sheets of tracing paper to "try on" ideas that you like from books, magazines, or gardens you've visited. Draw in beds, paths, fences, arbors, benches, and other details on the tracing paper. If you have trouble visualizing the garden from a bird's-eye view, sketch your ideas from the normal perspective. Don't worry about them being works of art; these sketches are for your eyes only.

As you think about structures for the garden, keep in mind the style of your home and its construction. The garden will blend into your landscape best if you build structures from materials that complement the materials already in use in your home and yard.

Once you decide on an overall plan, draw in bubbles to represent the plants you want to grow. Again, use sheets of tracing paper to experiment with plant combinations. To help

come up with combinations, consider the design principles that artists follow. These include repetition, contrast, and balance.

REPETITION is the reappearance of the same plant or a similar form, texture, or color throughout an area. For example, placing clumps of silvery lamb's-ears at regular intervals along the front of the garden is repetition, as is having a tall, silvery artemisia at the back of the bed. Repetition helps unify a design, pulling all the elements together.

CONTRAST, or the juxtaposition of opposites, adds interest to a design. You can contrast size, shape, foliage color, and texture; however, too much contrast creates a jumble. In the previous example, the artemisia's size contrasts with that of the lamb's-ears, so while unifying a design, it also adds interest.

BALANCE is the perception of stability in a design. A large standard at the corner of a bed would be balanced by an identical standard at the opposite corner for formal or symmetrical balance. A large anise hyssop can be balanced by a group of three small to medium-size herbs. This is informal or asymmetrical balance.

FORMAL GARDENS

In a formal garden design, all parts are symmetrically balanced. That is, each half of the garden is a mirror image of the other half. You can develop a formal herb garden in a myriad of shapes and sizes. However, they are most often geometrically shaped with straight lines.

At its most basic, the formal garden involves a central axis such as a broad expanse of lawn, a pathway, or a door, with identical plantings bordering the axis. This simple concept has been taken to elaborate extremes in the perennial borders found on magnificent estates in England. However, the results are no less spectacular on a small scale using herbs instead of flowers.

gardens. Although they evolved from medieval monastery gardens, they really have their roots in the intricately patterned parterre designs originating with the French in the 1500s, such as those at Versailles.

For convenience with these types of formal herb gardens, the width of each bed should be no more than 5 feet across so that you can easily reach its center from the path.

Besides symmetrical balance, most formal herb gardens are characterized by clean, straight lines. The plants are sheared or at least neatly pruned. Often the geometric beds are ringed by a short sheared hedge.

Paths, edgings, and focal points are other integral parts of symmetrically arranged

Neatly clipped borders add to the effect of the inherent symmetry of formal herb designs. Boxwood is the traditional hedging, but also try dwarf barberry or hyssop.

A popular style of formal herb garden is one whose area is divided into four or more geometric—square, rectangular, or triangular—beds separated by paths or lawn. This type of herb-garden design has evolved over time from the monastery and manor household gardens of the Middle Ages.

Another simple formal herb garden design is the wheel, where four or more wedge-shaped beds radiate from a central point. Sometimes gardeners use an old wooden wagon wheel to create the look of this small formal herb garden design. Rectangular beds skirting the perimeter of the centered-wheel garden are an adaptation of this design.

Knot gardens, see opposite page, are among the oldest and most traditional formal herb

formal herb gardens. Paths and edgings define the shape of beds, and they integrate color and pattern into the design.

PATHS: Brick is the traditional building material for paths in formal gardens, but flagstones, concrete pavers, and other similar materials work just as well. They all can be laid in a variety of patterns. Grass and gravel are other typical choices for making paths in formal gardens.

EDGING: Brick, stone, or wood are the best choices for edging formal beds because they create a rigidly straight line. Also available is molded concrete edging with tops formed into twists or rolls, scallops, and other shapes. Because of their geometric shape, these are especially appropriate for formal herb gardens.

FOCAL POINTS: A focal point in the center of the garden or at the end of a path draws attention. It can be a piece of sculpture, a well-grown topiary, or the more traditional birdbath, sundial, or fountain. Even though the focal point draws attention, most formal garden plantings are designed to direct your eye to the focal point. For example, the long line of hedges that line the beds along a path seems to narrow the perspective of the scene and move your eye toward the focal point.

OTHER FEATURES: A fence or neatly trimmed hedge surrounding a formal garden sets it apart and adds to the feeling of peace within an herb garden. Fences and hedges also help to intensify the fragrances of the herbs. A bench or other garden seating is another traditional part of formal herb-garden design.

MAINTENANCE

For a formal herb garden to truly work, you must maintain it rigorously. Keep the herbs neatly pruned and sheared, the walkways freshly swept, and the beds sharply edged.

The elaborate formal borders so often seen in British gardens can be translated on a simpler scale to your backyard. Use a hedge or a fence as the background. If the garden is wide, establish grass between the borders. Between narrow gardens, put a path. Include clipped evergreens to make the garden attractive year-round and a fountain, birdbath, or sculpture as a focal point.

KNOT GARDENS

In the Tudor era, 1485 to 1603, gardeners translated the intricate formal designs found in stitchery, laces, and plaster ceiling patterns to the garden. They planted herbs in elaborate loops and swirls. These became known as knot gardens.

A knot garden can be a time gobbler because you must prune the herbs several times during the growing season to maintain their shape and compact size. Still, a knot garden is a stunning addition to the landscape, especially if you locate it where it can be seen from above, such as from the top of garden stairs, a terrace, or from a window.

Traditional knot-garden plants are woody perennial herbs that can withstand frequent, light pruning and shaping. The herbs most often used to outline the knot garden include dwarf boxwood, lavender, dwarf barberry, hyssop, santolina, and germander. But don't overlook upright varieties of thyme, chives, or winter savory.

If you don't want the responsibility of a permanent knot garden, create one from compact annual herbs, such as dwarf globe basil, curly parsley, or bush nasturtiums. The more compact the plant, the less work will be required in the garden.

When planting a knot garden, set the herbs at half the spacing you normally would use in the garden. It's a good idea to have extra plants growing in pots to replace any that die.

For those with patience, a knot garden—whether simple or elaborate, large or small—brings visual rewards that make the effort worthwhile.

INFORMAL GARDENS

The entire space of an informal herb garden may be filled with plants. Stepping stones allow easy passage among the herbs.

Even though herb gardens traditionally have been formal in style, informal gardens are more easily adaptable to the style of modern homes.

Cottage gardens are the most elemental example of an informal garden. In a cottage garden, all kinds of plants fill the space in a riot of growth.

However, informal gardens don't necessarily have to be a wild-and-woolly jumble-like cottage gardens. More often, today's informal gardens are tidy borders or beds with curving edges and paths offset by lawn.

WHAT IS INFORMAL?

By definition, an informal garden design imitates nature. First, it has asymmetrical balance. With asymmetrical balance, if a line is drawn down the middle of the garden, the two halves appear very different.

EDGINGS

Even the most casual-looking herb garden benefits, both in appearance and maintenance, from having neatly defined edges, even when the edges are occasionally softened by creeping plants spilling over them. A simple way to achieve a well-defined edge is to remove a section of lawn around the perimeter of a bed or border with a special saw-blade tool, a spade, or a half-moon edger.

Edging can be used as a barrier to slow grass from creeping into the planting area, and vice versa. Brick is the most traditional barrier edging for herb gardens. Other good materials include stone, cast-concrete landscape edging, and wood.

Install edging at the same height as the lawn so that the mower runs over it. Or set it so that it sits above the lawn. You'll need to maintain this with a lawn trimmer.

Well-defined edges make the herb garden more beautiful as well as easier to maintain. A barrier edging, such as brick, slows grass from creeping into the beds.

Visually, though, each has equal "weight" or balance. It's the same as described on page 25. A large anise hyssop can be balanced by three small- to medium-size herbs. Though not identical, they have the same visual heft.

Second, unlike formal gardens, which have mainly straight-line geometrical shapes, informal gardens take nearly any form: round, square, oval, curving, rectangular, or free-form. Informal gardens also lack the rigidity of formal gardens. Plants grow into their natural form as well as spill over their boundaries.

PATHS, EDGINGS, AND FOCAL POINTS

As with formal gardens, paths, edgings, and focal points are integral parts of informal design. However, paths in informal gardens are more likely to curve rather than lie straight. And they are as likely to be made of irregularly shaped and placed stepping-stones as they are of bricks or flagstones laid in geometric patterns.

In informal gardens, edgings serve more to denote the outer boundary of the bed or border and to make mowing easier than to be a part of the design as in formal gardens.

Focal points, such as birdbaths, sculptures, benches, bee skeps (domed hives of twisted straw), or sundials, add interest to an informal herb garden just as they do in formal gardens. However, the plantings surrounding a focal point in an informal garden are less likely to lead your eye in its direction. For the best placement of a focal point in an informal garden, set it about one-third of the way along the length of the border. Or, put it in a small bed or border opposite a larger garden.

Informal herb borders and beds are particularly suited to mixed plantings of annual and perennial herbs, perhaps accompanied by herbal trees and shrubs. They are also easy to integrate throughout a yard. For example, herbal shrubs can be used in a foundation planting, fronted with annual and perennial herbs. A corner planting might include an herbal tree, such as ginkgo, underplanted with shade-tolerant herbs, such as woodruff.

Informal herb gardens imitate the curving lines and asymmetrical plantings of nature. Here, santolina, roses, and fennel integrate a perennial garden.

Use an inexpensive half-moon or saw-blade edging tool to neatly cut a shallow trench edge around beds.

Edgings that rise above the surrounding lawn or pathway range between 2 and 8 inches tall. The higher the edging, the sturdier it must be to hold soil, and the deeper it must be sunk into the ground. As an edging, wood has a soft, informal appearance. Choose long-lasting woods like cedar or redwood.

HERBS AS EDGING PLANTS

In choosing low-growing herbs for edging a bed or border, consider whether you want a plant that can be formally trimmed, one that is naturally compact, or one that casually drapes over the edge of the garden. In an informal garden, a combination of the latter two is the most attractive. Some of the best informal edging herbs include:

- Lavender
- Thyme
- Curly parsley.

INFORMAL GARDENS
continued

WALL PLANTINGS

High or low, a retaining wall is often a necessity in a garden, but it can seem severe in the landscape. Herbs provide several solutions for softening the appearance of a wall to turn it into an attractive element in the garden.

A curving stone pathway beckons you into the garden. As you walk along and step on the herbs, their scent is released from the lush plants beside the stones.

One solution starts when you build the wall. Leave niches between the stones, which you can fill with herbs to create a wall with texture, color, and fragrance. Another solution is to plant herbs along the wall's base. This helps tie the wall to its surroundings so it doesn't look so stark rising

Low-growing herbs, such as creeping thyme, are good choices for planting along the edges of raised beds or retaining walls. The cascading stems have a softening effect.

out of the ground. Finally, plant creeping herbs to cascade over the top of the wall.

Because conditions around a wall are often quite dry, choose herbs that withstand drought to plant around it. With a mortarless wall, herbs that self-seed freely expand the planting naturally.

To plant in niches, blend equal parts soil and compost. Water the plant, let it drain, then unpot it. Place it in the niche and fill in around its roots with the soil-compost mixture.

STEPPING STONES AND PATHS

Because so much of the pleasure we derive from herbs comes from close association with their textures and scents, pathways through the herb garden become an opportunity to touch and smell. Herbs also improve the appearance of the hard lines of a path or of stepping stones. One way to use herbs along a path is to plant ground-hugging herbs between stepping stones. The best herbs for this area include the various creeping thymes and chamomile. Set one plant between each stepping-stone.

You can also intersperse herbs in a solid brick or stone path by removing a few bricks or stones to create a planting space. Mix the soil in the planting space with an equal amount of compost. Plant the herbs, filling in with the soil-compost mix. Space the herbs far enough apart that the walkway is not obscured or in a spot where they'll be constantly trod upon.

Herbs sprawling onto the path from the bed or border bring a softened appearance to the garden. Some of the best herbs for this are lady's mantle, catnip, lavender, and lamb's-ears. To achieve a more formal appearance,

HERBS FOR WALL PLANTINGS

- Prostrate creeping rosemary
- Lemon thyme
- Caraway thyme
- Common thyme
- Wall germander
- Sweet marjoram
- Oregano
- Winter savoy
- Vining nasturtiums
- Lavender
- Pinks

choose upright, rounded, or compact plants, such as the tiny-leaved bush basils, curly parsley, chives, or santolina.

HERBAL LAWNS

An herbal lawn releases splendid fragrance with every footstep.

Although herbs cannot take a lot of foot traffic like a grass lawn can, even a small area can be a delight to the senses when strategically placed. It can work as a separate accent area within an herb garden or around the base of a design focal point such as a bench, fountain, or sundial.

Start with a small patch, clearing it of all other plants and preparing the soil well. You can expand it later, if desired. Speed the process by starting with small plants, spaced 6 inches apart. Water and weed regularly and do not walk on the lawn until the plants are well established.

How relaxing to wiggle your toes in a chamomile lawn with its signature scent. 'Treneague' is a nonblooming, compact cultivar.

HERBS FOR LAWNS

- 'Treneague' chamomile
- Pennyroyal
- Wild thyme
- Caraway thyme
- Woolly thyme
- Creeping thyme

A variation on the herbal lawn is the herbal seat. This one at Sissinghurst in England is of stone, but you could plant a wooden one.

THEME GARDENS

Herbs are appealing not only for their culinary, medicinal, and fragrant qualities, but also for their fascinating historical, geographical, legendary, and other associations. What may begin simply as a desire to grow a few herbs for cooking can quickly expand into an interest in herbs from

Nectar-rich herb flowers, such as borage, attract butterflies to the garden. But remember, before there's a butterfly there's a caterpillar. Learn to recognize this stage of the life cycle so that you don't destroy them.

other eras and cultures. Certainly, you can combine a great many herbs in one garden area, but often gardeners find themselves wanting to create separate areas with particular themes.

Theme gardens provide an outlet for special interests such as growing Chinese herbs, tropical herbs, herbs a Roman cook might have used, herbs for liqueurs, herbs for magic, herbs based on Culpeper's astrological signs, herbs associated with fairies, herbs for specific ailments, native North American herbs, a particular herb family or genus, biblical herbs, herbs from the works of Chaucer or Shakespeare, or herbs that attract bees and butterflies.

The following theme gardens illustrate some possibilities and inspire you. Whatever idea you choose to explore, research it well. The adventure of discovery will pay dividends many times over.

BIRD AND BUTTERFLY GARDENS

Birds bring melodious song and bug-catching ability to the herb garden, while both birds and butterflies offer the charm of movement and color. When planning an herb garden to attract birds and butterflies, choose plants

that offer food for these creatures. You also should provide water, as well as spots—such as hedge, tree, and shrub plantings—for nesting and shelter from predators, and areas for hibernating butterflies.

Food plants for butterflies supply a lot of nectar. These include yarrow, purple coneflower, rosemary, catnip, borage, summer and winter savories, thyme, chives, chamomile, anise hyssop, sage, fennel, poppies, valerian, and basil. Other high nectar producers are calendula, horehound, marsh mallow, sweet marjoram, oregano, mullein, and mints.

Don't forget that butterfly populations include caterpillars, and that their main diet is foliage. Grow enough herbs for both you and them. And don't use harmful pesticides around the butterfly garden.

Hummingbirds are nectar-loving creatures, too. Honeysuckle is among their favorite herbal foods, but they also favor bergamot, iris, and sage. Seed-bearing plants draw other birds to the garden. Include purple coneflower, poppies, sage, goldenrod, and sunflowers for them.

MEDIEVAL GARDENS

In medieval Europe, most herb gardening was done in monasteries for medicinal purposes and to distill oils for fragrance. Monks studied the usefulness of herbs and cataloged their findings in some of the earliest books on gardening. *Le Livre Rustican*, a fifteenth-century French volume on healing herbs, has colorful illustrations of the neat, orderly "physic" gardens from this era.

Medieval gardens were usually very simple and almost always surrounded by a high stone or brick wall, with beds set apart by brick or stone paths. Formal in style, a small medieval garden might include only four square beds, while a larger one could have rows of square beds, each devoted to plants for different ailments. Somewhere in the garden was a well or fountain as a source of water. One corner might have an herbal tree, such as a hawthorn, with a bench beside it.

The herbs first grown by monks were brought by the conquering Romans. Among these 200 or so herbs were borage, betony, fennel, parsley, rosemary, sage, and thyme.

A courtyard or a walled garden area is the ideal site for a medieval herb garden. Usually formal in design, the garden might simply be four beds of equal size, or it could be a more elaborate design.

The monks administered many of their medicines in the form of sweetened, spirit-based drinks, some of which survive today as commercial liqueurs. Among the herbs used in flavoring these tonics were angelica, anise, lemon balm, caraway, coriander, fennel, hyssop, mint, sweet cicely, sweet flag root, sweet woodruff, tansy, thyme, violets, and wormwood. When creating a historically accurate garden, remember that some of the herbs have since been found to be harmful when eaten, including foxglove and comfrey.

EARLY AMERICAN GARDENS

A variation of the fan-shaped herb gardens of the "old country," American settlers grew herbs in a goosefoot bed. It makes an unusual space to grow herbs near a back door. Think of the webbed foot of a goose to picture this small, easy design style. The concept also can be expanded to a larger area by creating a series of wedge-shaped beds with a bench at the narrow end and a grove of small herb trees or shrubs at the broad end.

To create a goosefoot garden, decide what dimensions you want to use, then prepare the soil. Remove 6 inches of soil from the area where the three to five brick or stone paths will radiate from the central point. Each path should be 2 feet wide. Put 4 inches of sand in the path areas, then lay bricks or stones on top of it. Fill gaps between each stone with more sand. You now

have created four to six wedge-shaped beds ready to plant.

If you try this theme garden, consider planting herbs native to North America. These include purple coneflower, tobacco (perhaps substituting an ornamental nicotiana), wild rose, such as *Rosa carolina*, California poppy, lobelia, goldenseal, bloodroot, and mayapple.

Alternatively, in keeping with the early American heritage of the goosefoot garden, consider the herbs produced and sold by the Shakers, who did much to perpetuate the knowledge of herbs in this country. These herbs include basil, borage, horehound, hyssop, marjoram, tansy, sage, and thyme.

Most early American settlers' gardens had to be fairly simple. One exception was the goosefoot garden with paths separating fan-shaped beds.

CONTAINER GARDENING

Growing herbs in containers is not new. Records show that ancient Greeks, Romans, and Egyptians grew bay, myrtle, and other herbs in clay pots, and the Moors of southern Spain used potted herbs lavishly in their courtyards. Gardens in the twelfth-century British, fifteenth- and sixteenth-century Italian, and Victorian and Edwardian ages all had them, too.

For today's busy lives, nothing beats having a tub of culinary herbs near the kitchen door. Even if you have plenty of garden space, herbs in containers add beauty to your yard. And for those whose gardening is confined to a balcony or patio, pots of herbs are indispensable.

To successfully grow herbs in containers, provide a fertile, fast-draining potting soil and keep it adequately watered and fertilized during the growing season. Be sure to meet the herbs' light requirements.

Container herb gardens are attractive and they bring herbal scents up close. Place them near the grill for convenient access. The container garden above includes lemon balm, sage, oregano, winter savory, and marigolds.

CONTAINERS

Container choice is a matter of personal preference, with each material having pluses and minuses. The only requirement for containers is that they have drainage holes. **TERRA-COTTA** pots have a natural beauty, but they are heavy and difficult to move. They also break. You must shelter these pots in winter to avoid freezing, cracking, and breaking.

WOOD also has the problem of weight, but it can stand up to winter weather. The longest-lasting wood containers are made from redwood or cedar. When growing herbs and other edible plants, don't use containers made from treated wood, which could leach chemicals into the soil.

PLASTIC CONTAINERS are a lightweight alternative to terra-cotta and wood. Prices range from cheap to expensive, and there are many sizes, styles, and colors to choose from.

Most individual herbs are best planted in pots that are 12 to 14 inches across. For mixed plantings, choose larger containers that are at least 24 to 36 inches across.

POTTING SOILS

There are many commercially available potting soils, some much better than others. Unfortunately, there is no way to determine quality by reading the label on the bag; ingredients are seldom listed. Ask other gardeners what they use or buy a small bag to test the soil. Pick up a small amount and make a ball in your hand. If it stays in a ball, it is too heavy for good herb growth. Try another brand.

One way to avoid the uncertainty of potting soils is to mix your own. Combine equal parts of topsoil, coarse perlite, compost or peat moss, and coarse sand. All of these ingredients are available at nurseries and garden centers. The topsoil and compost can come from your own yard. For outdoor use, topsoil does not need to be sterilized.

If you make your own soil, add fertilizer to it, following manufacturer's recommendations as to amounts. You might also want to mix in a cup each of bone meal and composted manure to a bushel of soil. Commercial potting soils often have fertilizer mixed in.

PLANTING

To plant herbs in containers, moisten the mix with warm or hot water. Fill the pot with soil, then plant the herbs at the same depth as they were in their pots. For herbs that do not transplant well, sow seeds directly into the pot.

Window boxes are a cheerful addition to a home. Choose ones that are at least 8 inches deep and fill them with herbs that trail, have colorful foliage, or have bright flowers.

STRAWBERRY JAR

A planting of herbs in a strawberry jar is spectacular. Cascading herbs planted in the individual pockets of the jar create the best effect. These include creeping thyme, pennyroyal, marjoram, oregano, and creeping rosemary. Place small upright-growing plants in the top, such as parsley, chives, short varieties of basil, or savory.

The challenge when growing in strawberry jars is to adequately water all the plants. The way to accomplish this is by inserting a piece of PVC plumbing pipe drilled with holes in the center of the jar. Then fill the pipe with pea gravel. This provides a conduit for the water to reach all the way to the bottom.

Cut 2-inch-diameter PVC pipe to the height of the strawberry jar. Set the pipe in the jar, mark the location of the planting pockets on it, then drill ³/₈-inch holes around it at those points. A spade bit works best.

Place the pipe in the center of the jar and fill it with pea gravel. Cover the pipe with plastic, then hold it in place while filling the jar up to the bottom pockets with potting soil. Tamp the soil to settle it.

Remove a plant from its pot, loosen its soil and roots slightly, then set the roots into the planting pocket. Tuck potting soil around the roots. Repeat until all the pockets are planted and the jar is filled.

WATERING AND FERTILIZING

Watering properly is crucial for container-grown herbs. The potting soil should not stay wet for long periods because many herbs like slightly dry conditions. But as temperatures rise and roots grow during the summer, soil can dry out in a day. It's best to check every morning and thoroughly soak the soil when the top inch or so is dry.

Because of the relatively small area for the roots and the frequent watering that washes nutrients away, it's important to fertilize regularly during the growing season. Slow-release fertilizers are convenient where hot climates make frequent watering necessary.

IN THE AUTUMN

Either allow container plantings of annual herbs to die in the fall or take them indoors. Perennial or woody herbs can come indoors and grow as houseplants. Or, you can allow them to go dormant, then overwinter them in a sheltered spot, such as an unheated garage, taking them outdoors again in the spring.

ORNAMENTAL HERBS

Any dedicated herb gardener values the ornamental qualities of herbs. Some herbs are so attractive that gardeners often plant them in flower borders and other parts of the landscape.

The following herbs bring grace and beauty to traditional herb gardens, flower beds and borders, and any spot in the landscape in which you'd like to plant them.

ORNAMENTAL HERBS

Angelica (*Angelica archangelica*) is a stately, architectural biennial with large globes of tiny flowers. *A. gigas* is similar but has purple-bronze foliage and flowers.

Anise hyssop (*Agastache foeniculum*) sports spikes of lavender flowers from late summer into fall. This bushy perennial, along with related species and varieties, also offers flowers in shades of apricot, peach, orange-red, or white.

Bergamot (*Monarda didyma*), also known as beebalm, is a perennial, blooming profusely in summer in shades of scarlet, burgundy, mauve, pink, or white. Select mildew-resistant varieties, such as 'Marshall's Delight' and 'Petite Delight'.

Bronze fennel (*Foeniculum vulgare purpureum*) towers over the garden with feathery bronze foliage, which provides contrasting texture in flower beds and borders. It is perennial.

Catmint (*Nepeta* species), related to catnip, forms low-growing, fine-textured mats with masses of spiky blue or purple flowers. This perennial makes a fine edging. Consider growing *N. × faassenii*, *N. nervosa*, *N. sibirica*, or *N.* 'Six Hills Giant'.

Fern-leaved tansy (*Tanacetum vulgare crispum*) forms low-spreading clumps of bright green, finely divided and curled leaves. It can be invasive but excels in tough conditions. It is perennial.

Feverfew (*Tanacetum parthenium*) is a short, branching perennial with daisylike flowers in summer. The cultivar 'Aureum' has golden foliage. Other varieties have double white or yellow flowers.

Foxglove (*Digitalis purpurea*) accents gardens with long spikes of tubular flowers in shades of pink and white. The blooms rise above mounds of leaves on this

biennial in late spring and early summer. Perennial species have yellow or white flowers.

Germander (*Teucrium chamaedrys*) is a low-growing, spreading, woody perennial with tiny, bright green leaves. It responds well to pruning.

Hyssop (*Hyssopus officinalis*) forms a low-growing, spreading mound of foliage. It is a fine-textured, woody perennial with spikes of blue-purple flowers in summer. Use it to edge a border. Some varieties have white, pink, or red flowers.

Lady's mantle (*Alchemilla mollis*) is a perennial that forms low mounds of velvety, scalloped-edged, bright green leaves with airy sprays of chartreuse flowers. Try this perennial as an edging for a path.

Germander's woody stems are readily pruned into a low hedge.

Meadowsweet (*Filipendula ulmaria*) sends up tall stalks topped with clusters of tiny, white, fragrant flowers in summer. Rosettes of finely divided dark green leaves anchor this perennial. Variegated golden-hued forms are also available.

Nasturtium (*Tropaeolum majus*) is an annual with round leaves and spurred, funnel-shaped flowers in shades of red, orange, yellow, or cream. There are low-growing, mounding and climbing nasturtiums, as well as ones with variegated leaves.

Oregano and marjoram (*Origanum* species and cultivars) are tender to hardy perennials with low, sprawling growth and small, pointed leaves. Small clusters of tiny rose-purple, pink, or white flowers cover the plants in summer. A number of varieties are ornamental, including *O.* 'Kent Beauty'; *O. rotundifolium*; *O. vulgare* 'Aureum', 'Variegatum', and 'Aureum Crispum', *O. majorana* 'Aureum' and 'Variegata'; *O. onites* 'Aureum'; *O. dictamnus* and *O. laevigatum* 'Herrenhausen'.

Pot marigold (*Calendula officinalis*) has daisylike, single or double, yellow to orange flowers. It is an annual.

'Herrenhausen' oregano blooms in midsummer.

Angelica gigas is a dramatic plant for the flower border.

Purple coneflower
(*Echinacea purpurea*) is a bushy perennial with pale to shocking-pink daisylike flowers in mid- to late summer. It also blooms in white.
Sage (*Salvia* species) offers hundreds of species and cultivars, with many forms. Typically, culinary sage is a low-growing, spreading woody perennial with gray-green leaves. Other forms have purple, gold-and-white variegated, or white-yellow-and-pink variegated leaves.

Purple-leaved sage combines well with other ornamentals.

Sweet rocket
(*Hesperis matronalis*), a short-lived perennial, readily self-sows after bearing spikes of mauve or white single or

Thymus serpyllum 'Coccineus' blooms freely in summer.

double flowers that are fragrant in the evening.
Sweet woodruff
(*Galium odoratum*) is a low-growing, spreading perennial with whorls of small leaves and starry white flowers in spring. It is an excellent ground cover for shade.
Thyme (*Thymus* species and cultivars) carpets the ground with tiny leaves and flowers in shades of pink, magenta, or white.

A great number of species and varieties of this perennial are grown as decorative plants, for either their golden or variegated foliage or their masses of flowers.
Yarrow (*Achillea millefolium*) offers feathery leaves and flat-topped clusters of small flowers in shades of pink or white.

Many new varieties are available in a broad range of colors, including apricot, salmon, and brick red. Related species and varieties have yellow to golden flowers.

SILVER HERBS

A special group of ornamental herbs have gray, silver, or white foliage. These plants soften the transitions between other plants, and catch the eye at dusk and in the moonlight. Some gardeners also like to use them in an area entirely by themselves or as companions to plants with white flowers. They are the basis for a white garden.

Silver-leaved plants like artemisia set off other plants.

Artemisia (*Artemisia* species): Bushy perennial, usually with finely divided leaves ranging from silvery green to almost white. Some, such as 'Silver King', are invasive. 'Lambrook Silver' and 'Powis Castle' are among the best artemisias.

Curry plant (*Helichrysum angustifolium*): Bushy, spreading, woody perennial with narrow silver leaves. It can be pruned into a formal edging. Although it blooms with clusters of yellow flowers, the flowers are not the plant's best quality. Other species of *Helichrysum* have rounded, silver leaves and cascading stems.
Lamb's-ears (*Stachys byzantina*): Low-growing, spreading perennial with heavily felted leaves and spikes of pink flowers. Some cultivars, such as 'Countess Helene von Stein', have larger leaves or do not flower.
Lavender (*Lavandula angustifolia*): Bushy, spreading, woody perennial with narrow gray-green leaves. A number of varieties have fragrant flowers in shades of purple, lavender, pink, and white. They are good for informal edging. Woolly lavender (*L. lanata*) has felted silver-gray leaves.
Pinks (*Dianthus caryophyllus, D. plumarius*): Low-growing, spreading perennial with slender gray-green leaves. A number of varieties offer fragrant flowers in shades of pink,

red, and white. Pinks are good for informal edging.
Rue (*Ruta graveolens*): Bushy perennial with fine-textured, rounded-lobed, blue-gray leaves and clusters of small, yellow flowers. Leaves of 'Jackman's Blue' are more distinctly blue than the species.
Santolina (*Santolina chamaecyparissus*): Bushy, rounded perennial with feathery gray leaves and yellow button flowers. Plants can be pruned into a formal edging.
Silver horehound (*Marrubium vulgare*): Bushy perennial with felty white stems and small, wrinkled downy, gray-green leaves and small white flowers.
Thyme (*Thymus pseudolanuginosus*): Mat-forming perennial with woolly gray leaves; good between stepping-stones. *T. doerfleri* is similar but is less hardy and has thin, hairy, gray leaves.
Yarrow (*Achillea* 'Moonshine'): Bushy perennial with feathery, gray leaves and flat clusters of bright yellow flowers. *A. grandifolia* is similar but with white flowers.

CULINARY HERBS IN THE GARDEN

To get the most benefit and pleasure from growing herbs, make them a part of your everyday life, not something reserved purely for special occasions. To do this, your herbs must be easy to get to. The ideal and traditional place for growing culinary herbs is right outside the door nearest the kitchen.

If you cook outdoors a lot, it's convenient to have some herbs planted near the deck or patio. Before you plant, though, remember that to grow well most culinary herbs must get at least six hours of sunlight and have well-drained. Try incorporating them into flower beds or borders.

One of the easiest ways to create a small culinary herb garden is to make a raised bed either 4 by 4 feet or 4 by 8 feet. Even in these small spaces, you'll be able to grow about one to two dozen different herbs. For many herbs, a single plant will supply plenty of harvest. But if you really like a particular herb, consider planting extras.

Have your herbs handy so you can can get to them at a moment's notice. You may want to plant them at your back door, with the vegetables, at a kitchen window, or anywhere else convenient and close at hand.

The vegetable garden is another logical place to plant herbs, especially the ones you want in quantity. In fact, some herbs are best started by direct seeding into the garden, so allow space for several 2- to 3-foot rows when planning your vegetable garden.

If space or sunshine is at a premium, containers offer an ideal alternative. A pot 18 to 24 inches in diameter can hold a number of small herb plants. Mix trailing and upright plants for the greatest effect.

Create a mini-garden by surrounding a large mixed container planting with smaller pots of various sizes containing individual herbs.

USING HERBS
IN THE KITCHEN

The most ordinary of foods can improve with the addition of fresh herbs. To substitute fresh for dried herbs, use twice as much fresh as dried. When trying out an herb that is new to you, taste just a bit to sample the flavor, then consider how to use it in different dishes.

Herbs have been used since ancient times to bring out the flavor in food. Because they are so easily grown, herbs have always been available to rich and poor alike. Likewise, cooking with herbs is not a mysterious or complicated process. It is as simple as harvesting a few stems of this and some leaves of that, then mincing them, if necessary, and adding them to the dish being prepared. And just as people worry less and less about what wine goes with what food, don't worry about hidebound rules of which herb to pair with a particular food.

Certainly, guidelines can be followed, particularly when first learning to cook with herbs. Some pairings have the weight of hundreds of years of tradition behind them. But, if an herb's flavor does not appeal to you, don't be afraid to try something else. The best way to acquaint yourself with the possibilities of using herbs is to taste the fresh herb by itself. If you don't like the flavor at this point, then you may not like a dish prepared with it. If you do like the flavor, think about how the character of this particular herb might complement or contrast with various foods.

When substituting fresh herbs for dried in a recipe, or vice versa, use about twice as much fresh as dried. As a very general guideline, start by adding about a teaspoon of fresh herbs to a main dish that serves four people. Then you can decide whether more or less would be better next time.

Try adding herbs to various dishes. Include whole small leaves or torn larger leaves, such as basil or mint, in a tossed green salad, or minced leaves in a vinaigrette. Sprinkle them on soup just before serving. Pasta sauces, casseroles, Crock-Pot meals, steamed or roasted vegetables, and grilled foods benefit from the flavors of herbs. Wonderful combinations of fruit juices are available now, but they are much better when steeped with a zesty herb such as lemon balm. Many herbs are good in desserts, too, even those herbs we typically associate with savory dishes.

Cooking with herbs really comes down to being willing to experiment and then getting into the habit of using them daily, because there is no limit to what they can enhance—with no fat and few calories.

RECIPES

HERB BLENDS

A quick and easy way to add salt- and fat-free flavor to your favorite dishes, especially in winter, is to use different mixtures of dried herbs. Create herb blends that emphasize different kinds of ethnic cooking, such as Italian, Mexican, Thai, or Indian. Or, customize seasonings for specific foods, such as vegetables, fish, or pork, or for certain types of dishes, such as soups, pastas, or casseroles.

The advantages of making your own herb blends are that you have control over the freshness of the herbs and you can mix them to your tastes. Most herbs yield more than enough for drying and using in several blends.

ITALIAN HERB BLEND: In a large bowl, combine 1 cup dried parsley, 1 cup dried basil, ½ cup dried oregano or marjoram, ½ cup dried minced onion, ¼ cup dried minced garlic, ¼ cup dried thyme, 2 tablespoons crushed dried mild chile peppers, and 2 tablespoons dried sage. Blend thoroughly. Store in airtight jars in a dark place.

Besides using in pasta and pizza sauces, try this Italian herb blend in hamburgers and meatballs, pasta salad with sun-dried tomatoes and artichoke hearts, or a casserole of eggplant, tomatoes, and roasted red peppers.

THAI HERB BLEND: In a large bowl, combine ½ cup dried Thai basil, ½ cup dried lemon basil, ¼ cup dried peppermint, ¼ cup dried cilantro, ¼ cup dried chives, 2 tablespoons dried lemon zest, 2 tablespoons dried minced lemongrass or lemon verbena, 2 teaspoons five-spice powder, and 2 teaspoons crushed dried mild chile peppers. Blend thoroughly. Store in an airtight jar in a dark place. Use this blend in marinades for grilled fish, stir-fries, or spring rolls.

ALL-PURPOSE SALT-FREE HERB SEASONING: In a large bowl, combine ½ cup dried dill, ½ cup dried minced onion, ⅓ cup toasted sesame seeds, 2 tablespoons dried thyme, 1 tablespoon dried marjoram, 1 tablespoon dried lemon verbena, 1 tablespoon lovage or celery seeds, 1 tablespoon dried minced garlic, and 1 teaspoon paprika.

In batches, grind all ingredients together in a mortar and pestle or spice grinder. Store in an airtight jar in a dark place. Put some into small shakers with large holes, keeping one in the kitchen and another on the dining table instead of a salt shaker.

Homemade blends of dried herbs have much more flavor than store-bought ones, plus they'll include the exact herbs you like and want. Give some as gifts, too.

HERB BLEND FOR SOUP: In a large bowl, combine ½ cup dried parsley, ¼ cup dried lemon thyme, 2 tablespoons dried marjoram, 1 tablespoon dried summer savory, 1 tablespoon dried lovage, 1 tablespoon dried rosemary, 1 tablespoon dried tarragon, and 1 tablespoon dried lemon verbena. Blend thoroughly. Store in an airtight jar in a dark place. This seasoning works with most soups or stews and is especially good when making stock.

As beautiful as herb vinegars are in a window, their flavor lasts longer when stored in the dark.

Opal Basil Vinegar 1994

HERB VINEGARS

The benefit of using herb vinegars in cooking is that they embellish and emphasize flavors in food with no fat and few calories.

Herb vinegars have a role in salad dressings, marinades, and pickled foods, but there are a lot more possibilities. Substitute herb vinegar for part of the wine in a recipe, or use it to deglaze a pan for a sauce. Flavor soups or stews by adding a tablespoon or so of vinegar near the end of cooking.

The technique for making herb vinegar couldn't be simpler, but there are some basic guidelines for getting the best results. First, be sure to choose a good-quality vinegar, such as cider, white- or red-wine, rice, champagne, or sherry vinegar. Flavor with just one herb or combine four or five that appeal to you. Besides herb leaves, consider seeds, spices, hot peppers, garlic, or shallots.

To make herb vinegar, gather the desired fresh herbs, then wash and dry. Place 1 cup of herb leaves and tender stems into a clean, dry quart jar. Add room temperature vinegar, either two cups or to fill, making sure all the leaves are submerged. Cover with a nonmetal lid or put plastic wrap over the top first, if using a metal lid. Store in a cool, dark place for two weeks before checking the flavor. If desired, let it steep for another week or two.

Strain out herbs and put the vinegar into clean small bottles, adding fresh herb sprigs for decoration. Cover tightly with a cork or plastic cap. Store in a dark place. One-half cup of dried herbs can be substituted for fresh herbs.

RED-WINE VINEGAR: Consider bay, garlic, garlic chives, ginger, horseradish, hot pepper, juniper berries, marjoram, oregano, parsley, rosemary, sage, savory, shallots, or thyme.

WHITE-WINE VINEGAR: Consider anise, anise hyssop, basil, borage, burnet, calendula petals, chervil, chives, cilantro, dill, fennel, garlic chives, ginger, lavender flowers, lemon balm, lemon verbena, lemongrass, lemon thyme, mint, marjoram, nasturtium, parsley, rose, geranium, rose petals, savory, or tarragon.

CIDER VINEGAR: Consider anise, anise hyssop, basil, bay, cilantro, dill, fennel, garlic, garlic chives, ginger, horseradish, hyssop, lovage, marjoram, mint, nasturtium, oregano, parsley, hot pepper, rosemary, sage, savory, shallots, or thyme.

HERB CHEESES

Cream cheese, ricotta cheese, fresh goat cheese, and homemade yogurt cheese, whether in high-fat, low-fat, or nonfat versions, all become luscious additions to meals and snacks when paired with herbs.

No offering is as simple—yet elegant—as an herb cheese served with slices of French bread, crackers, or a platter of raw vegetables. Or, experiment with herb cheese as a filling in omelets, crepes, or ravioli. And don't forget it for topping the humble baked potato.

To make an herb cheese, mix 8 ounces of fresh soft cheese with ¼ cup minced fresh herb leaves. Blend by hand or with a mixer. Put into an airtight dish and refrigerate for at least four hours before serving to allow flavors to blend.

If desired, add other ingredients besides herbs, such as minced olives, finely chopped toasted nuts, or drained and minced oil-cured sun-dried tomatoes.

Some delicious herb combinations to consider: chives, parsley, marjoram, basil, thyme, and garlic;

Try flavoring store-bought mustards with herbs.

arugula, borage, and burnet; jalapeños and cilantro; or sage and shallots.

To make a dessert herb cheese, add 2 tablespoons honey or sugar to 8 ounces of cheese and concentrate on the "sweeter" herbs such as angelica, cinnamon basil, lavender, lemon thyme, mint, or sweet cicely. Minced dried fruit, such as cranberries, cherries, or apricots, or finely chopped toasted nuts are other good additions to dessert cheese.

HERB MUSTARDS

Mustard has been a popular condiment since the ancient Romans. With worldwide appeal, some form of mustard is found in or on everything from all-American hot dogs and hamburgers to Welsh rarebits, French vinaigrettes, Italian preserved fruits, and Chinese spring rolls.

Many herbs are a natural embellishment to the piquancy of mustard. Some to try, singly or in combination, include chives, cilantro, dill, garlic, horseradish, mint, parsley, rosemary, sage, shallots, tarragon, and thyme.

Although it's reasonable to make your own mustard by starting with the seeds themselves, there is such a range of commercially prepared mustards available that it makes more sense to focus your efforts on flavoring these with your choice of herbs.

To flavor a prepared mustard with your choice of herbs, combine ½ cup mustard with your choice of minced fresh or dried herbs, using about 2 tablespoons fresh or 1 tablespoon dried.

Store your herb-flavored mustard in an airtight container in the refrigerator for at least 8 hours before serving to blend flavors.

YOGURT CHEESE

Yogurt cheese indulges a desire for a tangy cheese spread yet also has yogurt's benefits. It's easy to make— only a thin cotton kitchen towel or several layers of cheesecloth are needed (or use a cloth strainer made for this purpose). Start  with homemade or store-bought plain yogurt, either whole-milk, low-fat, or nonfat; be sure to choose a brand that doesn't contain gelatin. (For a dessert cheese, use vanilla yogurt.)

To make homemade yogurt cheese, pour 1 quart yogurt into the yogurt strainer or a bowl lined with cloth. If using cloth, gather the corners and tie firmly. Suspend the bag over a bowl and let drip for at least four hours in the refrigerator. Save the whey for liquid when baking.

One quart of yogurt makes about 2 cups, or 1 pound, of cheese. Store in an airtight container in the refrigerator for up to a week.

COMBINATIONS

■ Coarse Dijon mustard with parsley, thyme, oregano, and garlic
■ Honey mustard with cilantro, ginger, and lemongrass
■ Dijon mustard with chervil and tarragon

RECIPES
continued

HERB SUGARS, SYRUPS, AND HONEYS

Satisfy your sweet tooth and get the flavors and fragrances of herbs at the same time with herb sugars, syrups, and honeys. They bring a fascinating dimension to iced or hot teas, lemonade, or desserts.

Herb sugar

Herb syrups are simply wonderful when poured on pancakes. Bake with flavored honey or whip it with butter for a luscious spread on breads or muffins.

Some of the best herbs for use in flavoring sugars, syrups, and honeys are the flowers of roses, clove pink, lavender, bergamot, pineapple sage, anise hyssop, mint leaves, scented geranium, lemon verbena, basil (especially cinnamon and lemon), thyme (especially lemon), fennel, sweet cicely, and angelica.

To make herb sugars, layer fresh or dried herb leaves or flowers with granulated sugar in an airtight container. Stir daily to keep the sugar from clumping.

Once the sugar stays dry and loose, remove the remaining large pieces of the leaves or the flowers, or grind the entire sugar-herb mixture in a food processor.

Herb honey

To make herb syrup, bring 3 cups of water to a boil. Remove from heat and stir in 1 cup of fresh or ½ cup dried herb leaves or flowers. Cover and steep for 30 minutes. Strain and return liquid to the pan. Stir in 2 cups sugar. Bring to a boil and cook for 10 minutes. Cool, bottle, and store in refrigerator.

To make herb honey, stir together 3 parts honey to 1 part fresh or dried herb leaves or

flowers, making sure the herbs are totally submerged. Steep in a tightly closed container for one to three weeks, or until the flavor is as desired. Strain to remove the herbs, then store in tightly capped jars.

HERB JELLIES

Herb jellies give a new dimension to peanut butter and jelly sandwiches, as well as biscuits, toast, or muffins. They also make flavorful fillings for tea sandwiches when combined with butter or cream cheese, and they become a sweet and savory condiment for roasted or grilled meats.

Your choice of herbs for flavoring jelly depends on your own preferences. Some of the more popular include thyme, lemon thyme, any of the mints or basils, lemon balm, sage, and tarragon. The simplest base for the jelly is water, but fruit juice or wine also can be used.

To make herb jelly, place 1 to 2 cups of fresh or dried herb leaves, flowers, or roots or up to ⅓ cup herb seeds in a large bowl. The amount of herbs used depends on the intensity of the herb and the desired flavor. Pour 1½ cups boiling water or other liquid over the herbs. Cover and let steep for 30 minutes. Strain and measure the liquid, adding water, if necessary, to yield 1½ cups.

Pour the herb liquid into a large, heavy, nonreactive pan. Stir in ½ cup vinegar, preferably flavored with herbs, and 3½ cups sugar. (When using fruit juice as a liquid, vinegar is not used.) Cook over high heat,

HOW TO MAKE A TEA COZY WITH MATCHING MUG MATS

Purchase a quilted place mat and a matching or complementary napkin. To make the tea cozy, fold the mat in half, matching the shorter ends. Cut the mat on the fold. Hem each piece using bias tape. Place the two halves together, right side out, and whipstitch them together. To make the mug mats, cut four pieces from the napkin, each 4½ by 8 inches. Fold each piece in half, right sides together, matching shorter ends. Sew two sides together, using a ½-inch seam allowance. Trim the corners and turn right side out. Fill loosely with dried herb leaves or crushed spices. Whipstitch remaining side shut.

stirring, until the mixture comes to a full rolling boil. Stir in 3 ounces of liquid pectin. Continue cooking and stirring until the mixture again reaches a full rolling boil that can't be stirred down. Cook for one minute, stirring constantly. Remove from heat and skim off any foam from the surface. Ladle into hot sterilized half-pint canning jars, leaving ¼-inch headspace. Wipe the rims and attach two-piece canning lids. Follow the standard directions for the boiling-water method of preserving, boiling the jars for five minutes.

HERB CORDIALS

From their medieval origins as medicines produced in monasteries, cordials and liqueurs flavored with herbs have made their way to our homes as commercially produced products, such as Chartreuse or Benedictine. Making your own aperitif or after-dinner herb cordial is simple and easy, and it allows you to pick and choose from among your favorite herbs.

Among the herbs for cordials, consider angelica, anise, bay, caraway, coriander, cumin, fennel, hyssop, lavender, lemon balm, lemon verbena, mint, rose, rosemary, saffron, sage, sweet cicely, sweet woodruff, tarragon, thyme, and violet. Spices such as cinnamon sticks, cardamom pods, whole cloves, allspice berries, peppercorns, and star anise may also be used as flavorings for liqueurs and cordials.

A basic method for making an herb cordial is to combine a fifth of vodka, brandy, rum, or whiskey with 2 to 3 cups of fresh herb leaves or flowers or up to ½ cup lightly crushed seeds or spices in a large jar with a tight-fitting lid. Let steep in a dark place for four to six weeks. Strain and combine with a sugar syrup made with 2 cups sugar and 1 cup water, after the syrup has cooled. Bottle your cordial, then let the flavors blend for several more weeks.

HERB TEAS AND DRINKS

For centuries, herb teas have been used for their curative properties, but they also are enjoyed simply for their flavor. And what could be easier!

Pour boiling water over dried or fresh herbs (1 teaspoon to 1 tablespoon per cup of water), then let it infuse for 5 to 10 minutes. Drink the fragrant result hot or cold.

Calorie-free and usually without caffeine as well, herb teas offer subtle, delicate flavors that can be enjoyed any time of day. Create other herbal beverages by steeping herbs with fruit juices, wines, or other drinks. For example, intensify the flavor of lemonade with lemon balm or lemon verbena. Try pineapple sage, mint, or ginger with tropical juices like pineapple or papaya. Add ginger mint to a glass of ginger ale. Rosemary enhances cranberry juice, while sage or thyme pairs well with apple or grape juice. Celery-flavored lovage is, of course, the perfect partner to tomato juice. Sweet herbs such as angelica or sweet cicely tone down the tartness of grapefruit juice without adding calories.

Sweet woodruff and riesling wine are a traditional combination in may wine. Add lemon balm, lemon verbena, or lemon thyme leaves to make an herbal red- or white-wine sangria. Rosemary and orange mint both are good choices as additions to mulled wine.

Make your own flavored black tea by adding dried flowers and leaves to a canister of black tea. The tradition of adding dried jasmine flowers is long-standing, but hibiscus or orange flowers, rose petals, or mint leaves are other possibilities.

Finally, don't forget to add some herbal flowers when making ice cubes. Use any edible flower, such as borage, rose petals, mint, thyme, rose geranium, violets or lavender. Put one flower, petal, or sprig into each section of an ice cube tray, then fill half way with water and freeze. Fill completely with water and freeze again.

INSTRUCTIONS FOR BOILING-WATER BATH

Fill a large, deep kettle half full of boiling water. Place filled, lidded canning jars into the kettle, leaving at least 1 inch between jars. Add more boiling water to the kettle, covering the lids by 2 inches. Cover the pot, bring to a hard boil, and boil for the recommended time, lowering heat slightly, if necessary. Remove the jars from the boiling water. Cool, remove bands, label, and store in a cool, dark place.

Lemon verbena tea not only refreshes on a hot day, but adds a touch of elegance. And it's easy to prepare.

MEDICINAL HERBS IN THE GARDEN

There is comfort and security in being able to go out into the garden to cut a few herbs to make a soothing tea for a headache or an ointment for a cut. Growing your own medicinal herbs offers the assurance of ready access, freshness, and purity. Because many of the familiar culinary herbs also have therapeutic qualities, with a little forethought and planning, a small herb garden can do double duty for both cooking and curing. In addition, many medicinal herbs are familiar flowers, shrubs, trees, or vines that can be incorporated throughout the landscape naturally and gracefully.

For fast and easy access, consider creating an area near the house that is specifically for the medicinal herbs you use most often. A 4- by 15-foot garden or raised bed provides enough space for a wide range of plants. Most medicinal herbs require full sun, just like their culinary counterparts, so choose a spot with full sun. Herbs can adapt to a wide range of soil types, as long as they are well-drained. Incorporate compost or rotted manure before planting and provide a mulch to control weeds and conserve moisture.

A wide range of herbs can improve both health and appearance. Some of these are among the familiar, like lavender, and others are more exotic, like goldenseal or ginseng.

USING HERBS
FOR HEALTH & BEAUTY

Homemade herbal medicines, as well as facial and body care preparations, offer an opportunity for better health simply and naturally.

The power of plants to cure, heal, and improve appearance has been used by humankind from the earliest times. Only in the last hundred years or so have we come to rely more on medicines that come from a laboratory rather than from the landscape. During the last quarter of the twentieth century, there has a been a resurgence of interest in using plants for better health.

People are looking at ways to prevent health problems and to treat minor ailments without using potent medications. Among alternative treatments is phytotherapy—the use of plants to prevent and treat disease. Fruits, vegetables, and herbs can function preventively. For example, it has been claimed that tomatoes and broccoli protect against some forms of cancer, that basil prevents ulcers, and that horseradish removes toxins from the body.

Phytotherapy also refers to use of plants in treating existing conditions, such as fennel and lemon balm tea for indigestion or nettle shampoo for dandruff. Using herbs for face, body, and hair care offers natural, inexpensive ingredients without damaging preservatives.

The remedies in this book are based on observation and tradition—not on rigorous scientific testing. Some of the plants have not been analyzed for their chemical content. Also, potency of plant chemicals vary from plant to plant, so remedies may vary in potency from one batch to the next.

Although most medicinal herbs are safe when used as recommended, any substance, however natural, can be dangerous if used in excess. In learning to use herbs for health, become familiar with the ways that herbs can be prepared and with the specific benefits of various herbs and keep these ideas in mind:

■ Do not use herbs to treat major or long-standing medical conditions.

■ If you are taking prescription medicines, consult a doctor before taking any herbal preparation.

■ Take no more than one internal remedy at a time because chemicals from different plants may interact. Start with small amounts and monitor yourself for allergic reactions.

■ Pregnant or nursing women should use *only* herbs specifically recommended as safe for their condition.

MAKING HERBAL REMEDIES

Most herbal remedies are simple to make, requiring equipment that is already in the kitchen. Use enamel, stainless-steel, glass, pottery, or cast-iron utensils, but never aluminum. Wash utensils with hot soapy water, then rinse and dry before use. Glass jars or bottles are best for storing herbal remedies. Clearly label all ingredients and preparations. When fresh herbs are not available, use one-third to one-half as much of dried herbs, depending on the preparation.

INFUSION: An infusion is a tea made from fresh or dried leaves, flowers, or soft stems of herbs and used internally or externally for a wide range of conditions. To make an infusion, warm a teapot with hot water, drain, and add 1 ounce dried or 3 ounces fresh herbs. Pour in 2¼ cups water that has just begun to boil. Cover and infuse for 10 minutes. Strain. Take up to three 6-ounce doses daily, hot or cold, adding honey or sugar, if desired. Store unused infusion in the refrigerator for up to two days.

DECOCTION: This is a tea made from fresh or dried bark, berries, seeds, or roots of herbs and used internally or externally for a wide range of conditions. Bark or berries should be crushed and roots washed, scraped, and chopped or grated. Combine 1 ounce dried or 2 ounces fresh herbs with 3 cups cold water in a saucepan. Bring to a boil, reduce heat, and simmer gently for 20 to 40 minutes, or until volume has reduced by about one-third. Strain through a jelly bag, squeezing tightly. Take up to three 6-ounce doses daily, hot or cold, adding honey or sugar, if desired. Store unused portion in the refrigerator for up to two days.

SYRUP: A syrup is a double-strength infusion or decoction of fresh or dried herbs, sweetened with honey or sugar, then cooked to a syrupy consistency. A syrup is taken internally, most often for coughs. To make a syrup, follow directions for an infusion or decoction, using half as much water. In a clean saucepan, combine 1 cup of the strained liquid with ⅓ cup honey or ½ cup sugar. Simmer gently, stirring occasionally, until the mixture thickens. Cool, then pour into sterilized, dark glass bottles. Insert a cork stopper, then label and store in refrigerator up to three months. Take 1 to 2 teaspoons no more than three times a day.

TINCTURE: A tincture is a solution made by steeping any part of an herb in a mixture of alcohol and water. It is used internally or externally for a wide range of conditions. Quantities vary according to each herb, but a general guideline is to use 2 ounces dried or 6 ounces fresh herbs with 1 cup of 75-proof vodka and ½ cup water. Place herbs, vodka, and water in a glass jar, cap tightly, and store for three weeks, shaking vigorously every other day. Strain and pour into sterilized, dark glass bottles. Cap tightly, label, date, and store for up to two years. Take up to three doses daily, diluting 1 teaspoon in a little warm water.

OIL: An oil is an extraction of herbs in a vegetable oil, such as safflower or sunflower, for external uses as massage oils, creams, and ointments. Herbal oils made from flowers are usually cold infused, while those from leaves are best prepared by hot infusion. To make a cold-infused oil, pack a quart glass jar with the fresh or dried herb. Cover with the oil. Cap tightly and place on a warm, sunny windowsill for two weeks, shaking each day. Strain through a jelly bag, squeezing hard, then repeat with more herbs. After two weeks, strain again and pour into sterilized, dark glass bottles. Cap tightly, label, and refrigerate for up to a year. To make a hot-infused oil, combine 8 ounces dried herbs with 2 cups oil in the top of a double boiler. Set over simmering water and heat gently for three hours, taking care not to let the lower pan boil dry. Cool. Strain through a jelly bag, squeezing hard. Pour into sterilized, dark glass bottles. Cap tightly, label, and store in a dark, cool place for up to a year.

OINTMENT: An ointment is an extraction of fresh or dried herbs in white petroleum jelly used externally for bruises or skin conditions. To make an ointment, slowly heat 1 cup of petroleum jelly in the top of a double boiler over simmering water. When melted, stir in 1 ounce dried or 3 ounces fresh herbs. Heat gently for two hours, taking care not to boil dry. Strain through a jelly bag, pressing against the bag with a wooden spoon. Quickly pour the strained mixture into sterilized, dark glass jars. Cap tightly, label, refrigerate or store in a dark, cool place for up to four months.

POULTICE: A poultice uses fresh or dried herbs that are applied directly to the affected external part of the body. To make a poultice, pour boiling water over crushed or chopped herbs. When just cool enough to handle, remove herbs from liquid, squeezing out excess water. Spread herbs on the affected area and wrap with gauze to hold the poultice in place.

COMPRESS: A compress is a cloth soaked in an herb infusion or decoction, then applied to the affected body part. Soak a clean piece of soft cotton fabric, such as muslin, in the herb liquid. Squeeze out the excess, fold into a pad, and place on the area, repeating until relief is felt. The liquid can also be made by mixing 2½ tablespoons of tincture in 2 cups hot or cold water. Cold compresses are best for headaches, black eyes or bruising.

CHOOSING HERBS FOR COMMON AILMENTS

Properly administered, herbal remedies offer an alternative to conventional pharmaceutical drugs, especially for relief of minor ills. However, "natural" herbs hold the potential for misuse, just as with any drug. Never exceed the prescribed dosage. If there is no improvement after a reasonable amount of time, seek professional help. Because of the vast numbers of plants in the world, there are many more medicinal herbs than can be mentioned here or in the encyclopedia section. This book seeks to emphasize the safest, most easily grown and used herbs.

ARTHRITIS: To seek relief from joint pain, inflammation, and swelling, drink a decoction made from 2 teaspoons of fresh gingerroot. An infusion of oregano, rosemary, and basil, all with high antioxidant properties, may also be beneficial.

BAD BREATH: For an herbal mouthwash, use a tincture or infusion made with rosemary, sage, peppermint, spearmint, basil, tarragon, lemon verbena, fennel, bergamot, lavender, hyssop, anise seeds, cilantro, tansy, or yarrow, combining several different herbs, if desired. Chew fresh parsley or anise or fennel seeds.

BRUISES, MUSCLE STRAINS, AND SPRAINS: Apply a poultice of arnica or comfrey directly on the bruise. Use a compress of parsley or St. John's wort for sprains. Rub an arnica or St. John's wort ointment into the bruised area.

BURNS: Use a home treatment only for first-degree burns, such as an ordinary sunburn, or for second-degree burns with blisters no larger than a quarter. All other burns should receive immediate medical attention. Break open an aloe leaf and apply directly to the burn, or apply an oil or ointment made from lavender, St. John's wort, calendula, honeysuckle, or elder flowers. Use a poultice or compress of plantain leaves, angelica, or salad burnet. Herbal vinegar made from any of the above herbs is also soothing.

COLDS AND FLU: At the first sign of a cold or flu, try drinking a decoction of purple coneflower or gingerroot, continuing until well. Add raw garlic to broth, preferably one made with lots of onion, ginger, and hot red pepper. Other possibilities include an infusion of forsythia seeds, honeysuckle flowers, and lemon balm leaves. Other beneficial herbs to use in infusions include agrimony, eyebright, fennel, or sage leaves. Aniseed infusion acts as an expectorant.

CONSTIPATION: The first line of defense is to eat five fruits and five vegetables a day, while reducing low-fiber foods from the diet. Among the readily available, easily grown herbs useful as a gentle laxative are basil, dandelion, parsley, or feverfew leaves. Use as an infusion. If constipation is accompanied by lower abdominal pain or painful defecation, consult a physician.

COUGHS: Make an infusion of sage, thyme, and gingerroot; then add lemon juice and honey, which are beneficial for any of the teas suggested for coughs. Also consider a decoction of marsh mallow or elecampane root or an infusion of mullein or cowslip flowers or white horehound leaves. Angelica syrup is generally soothing. For phlegmy chest coughs, try a syrup made from licorice root, thyme and lungwort (*Pulmonaria* spp.) leaves, cowslip flowers, and aniseed. Do not use licorice root for longer than two weeks. For a dry cough with a runny nose and head cold, try an infusion of boneset, yarrow, and peppermint leaves and elder flowers. Seek medical attention if the cough persists more than a week.

CUTS AND ABRASIONS: Wash wounds with a calendula infusion or tincture added to water. Use an ointment or compress of calendula, St. John's wort, or comfrey. Make a tincture with horsemint or with a combination of thyme, rosemary, mint, and wintergreen.

DIARRHEA: Drink plenty of fluids and choose herbs high in tannin—to reduce inflammation—and high in mucilage to add bulk to the stool and soothe the digestive system. Drink an infusion of high-tannin agrimony, blackberry, or raspberry leaves, combined with a decoction of soothing, mucilaginous marsh mallow root. Consult a physician immediately if diarrhea is accompanied by blood in the stool, bouts of lower abdominal pain, fever of 100° F or greater, or vomiting. Do not treat children with home remedies for diarrhea—consult a medical reference book for further symptoms that require consultation with a physician.

Rosemary is a traditional remedy for arthritis, bad breath and cuts. Be aware that although natural, herbs can be misused, just as with any drug. Before using, accurately identify the complaint and choose the safest, mildest herb and treatment for the problem. One advantage to using home-grown herbs in homemade preparations is the assurance of their freshness and purity.

CHOOSING HERBS FOR COMMON AILMENTS
continued

For most minor problems, the remedy is drinking an herbal tea, technically called an infusion. Dill tea helps relieve indigestion and flatulence.

EYE STRAIN: Lie down and place a cold compress over eyes, using an infusion of eyebright, vervain, or hyssop leaves, or the flowers of chamomile or mullein.

FEVER: There are probably more herbs for reducing fever than for any other malady. Wait to treat a fever until you're uncomfortable because a fever is a natural body defense. Drink an infusion of catnip, vervain, and boneset for the hot, sweaty stage of a fever and a decoction of gingerroot and cinnamon for chills. Drinking an infusion of meadowsweet flowers or a decoction of willow bark can also help to reduce a fever. Children and people allergic to aspirin should not use meadowsweet or willow. For a fever of 103° F or higher or any fever that lasts more than two days, consult a doctor immediately.

FLATULENCE: A number of herbs have carminative properties that minimize this disturbance, including anise, basil, bergamot, caraway, chamomile, cilantro, dill, fennel, garlic, ginger, hyssop, lavender, lemon balm, marjoram, oregano, peppermint, rosemary, sage, savory, tarragon, and thyme. A soothing after-dinner tea might be an infusion of chamomile flowers, fennel seeds, and lemon balm and peppermint leaves.

HEADACHE: There are various kinds of headaches, and no one herb works on all of them. For migraines, try an infusion of fresh feverfew leaves and fresh or dried bay leaves. (Pregnant women should *not* use these herbs.) For general headaches, drink an infusion or decoction made from an herb with aspirinlike qualities, such as willow bark, meadowsweet flowers, or wintergreen leaves. Children and those allergic to aspirin should not use these herbs. Some other herbs that are believed good in infusions for headaches include lemon balm, peppermint, rosemary, sage, or thyme leaves and lavender, chamomile, or linden flowers. Rub lavender or peppermint oil on temples.

INDIGESTION: Try infusions made from anise, caraway, coriander, or dill seeds or angelica, lemon balm, or mint leaves, or chamomile or linden flowers, either singly or in some combination. Chew dill, anise, or fennel seeds. If indigestion leads to vomiting, feeling faint, passing dark stools, or abdominal pain, consult a physician.

INSECT BITES AND STINGS: For an insect repellent, rub mountain mint or pennyroyal leaves on skin and clothing. To relieve pain from minor bites and stings, apply fresh calendula petals, plantain leaves, garlic clove, or onion slice directly, or as a poultice.

INSOMNIA: About 45 minutes before bedtime, drink an infusion of lemon balm, California poppy, passionflower, bergamot, elder flower, wood betony, chamomile, catnip, or hops, either singly or in combination. Or, make a decoction of valerian root and drink cold. Stop after three weeks and do not use again for at least one week.

MENSTRUAL CRAMPS: Drink an infusion of raspberry leaves or a decoction of Chinese angelica roots or blackhaw bark.

MUSCULAR ACHES AND PAINS: Apply bay, elecampane, horseradish, or wintergreen oil or ointment and massage lightly.

NAUSEA: Try an infusion of gingerroot, basil, cinnamon bark, peppermint, or lemon balm leaves, or fennel seeds. If vomiting, consult a medical reference book for symptoms that require consultation with a physician.

SORE THROAT: Use a gargle made of an infusion or tincture made with sage, rosemary, lady's mantle, marsh mallow, wintergreen, agrimony, aniseed, ginger, or garlic, used singly or in combination. Use a honeysuckle flower syrup.

CHOOSING HERBS FOR FACIAL CARE

NORMAL SKIN: Anise, calendula, chamomile, comfrey, dandelion, elder, lavender, lemon balm, lemongrass, sage, yarrow

DRY SKIN: Anise, borage, chamomile, comfrey, dandelion, elder, fennel, lemon balm, lemongrass, marjoram, marsh mallow, parsley, red clover, rose

OILY SKIN: Anise, bay, bergamot, borage, calendula, catnip, comfrey, dandelion, elder, fennel, lavender, lemon balm, lemongrass, marjoram, parsley, peppermint, plantain, raspberry, red clover, sage, thyme, yarrow

WRINKLES: Fennel, lemon balm, linden

ROUGH SKIN: Elder, salad burnet

BROKEN VEINS: Borage, calendula, chamomile, rose

MATCHING OIL TO SKIN TYPE

NORMAL SKIN: Almond, canola, corn, grape-seed, peanut, sesame, sunflower, safflower.

DRY SKIN: Almond, canola, cocoa butter, grape-seed, olive, peanut

OILY SKIN: Soy

FACIAL CARE

FACE PACKS: Use once a week to deep cleanse, nourish, soothe, and smooth the skin.

For normal skin, combine 3 tablespoons of an infusion made from any of the herbs suggested for normal skin, 2 tablespoons plain yogurt, 3 tablespoons oatmeal or wheat germ, and 2 tablespoons honey.

For oily skin, combine ½ cup of any of the herbs for oily skin in a blender with ¼ cup water and puree. Add 1 egg white, and mix.

For dry skin, combine 2 teaspoons almond oil, 1 egg yolk, 1 tablespoon brewer's yeast, and 2 tablespoons of a strong infusion made from any of the herbs for dry skin.

For all skin types, combine 2 teaspoons each of arrowroot thickener and honey in a small saucepan, then stir in ¾ cup herb infusion, choosing from among the herbs for your skin type. Cook over medium heat, stirring until thickened. Cool and stir in 1 teaspoon herb oil. This keeps well for several months if stored in a refrigerator in a tightly capped jar.

To use, first wash your face thoroughly with a pure soap, rinse with lukewarm water, and pat dry. Smooth on the face pack mixture, avoiding lips and eyes. Lie down and rest for 15 minutes. Rinse the pack off with lukewarm water and pat dry. Smooth on moisturizer.

FACIAL STEAMS: Another method of deep cleansing and softening skin is with a facial steam. Use ¼ cup dried or ½ cup fresh herbs with 1 quart boiling water, selecting herbs according to skin type (see page 48).

First cleanse your face with a cleansing lotion or cream, then wash with soap and lukewarm water. Rinse and pat dry. People with very dry skin should apply a thin coat of facial oil. Combine the herbs and boiling water in a large bowl. Lean over the bowl and cover your head with a towel to hold in the steam. Remain over the steam for about 10 minutes. Gently wipe face with a damp cloth, then apply a freshening lotion. Do not go outside for at least an hour.

SKIN CLEANSERS: Use cleansers twice a day to remove dirt, makeup, and dead cells, as well as to soften skin. Smooth a cream or lotion over skin, then gently wipe it off with a tissue. Follow with a further cleansing, using a mild soap and lukewarm water.

The simplest cleanser to make at home is a cleansing oil. Follow the directions for herb-infused oil (see page 46), using one of the oils recommended for your skin type (see page 48).

For those who prefer a cream, combine 2 tablespoons lanolin, or coconut or shea butter (a fat from Africa's shea tree available from natural-foods stores) with ½ ounce grated beeswax in the top of a double boiler over simmering water. When melted, slowly whisk in ½ cup of oil recommended for your skin type. Remove from heat and whisk in 2 tablespoons herb infusion.

FRESHENING LOTIONS: Follow skin cleansing with a freshening lotion to remove the last traces of dirt and cleanser. Freshening lotions also soothe, heal, and refresh the skin. The simplest freshening lotion is an infusion made with 1 tablespoon fresh or 2 teaspoons dried herbs for each cup of boiling water, choosing herbs according to skin type. Let steep for 30 minutes, strain, and bottle. To use, moisten a cotton ball with the lotion and gently wipe face.

MOISTURIZERS: The final step in skin care is to apply a moisturizer, which slows moisture loss from skin and protects it from weather, pollutants, and dry indoor air. A simple herbal moisturizing lotion can be made by combining ¼ cup herbal infusion, matching herb to skin type, with 2 tablespoons glycerin or lanolin.

LIP BALM: To keep lips soft and smooth, as well as to soothe and heal chapped lips, use a lip salve. To make, combine ½ ounce grated beeswax with 1½ teaspoons cocoa or shea butter in the top of a double boiler placed over simmering water. When melted, stir in ¼ cup calendula herb oil. Remove from heat and cool to lukewarm, then stir in 1 teaspoon glycerin and several drops of your favorite essential oil, if desired. (To test for a reaction to the oil, put a dab on your wrist before using on your lips.) Pour into small jars.

NOTE: Extended use of lavender or yarrow can cause skin to become sensitive to sunlight, causing uneven pigmentation.

Homemade facial care preparations can be tailored to your skin type. For example, sage is good for normal or oily skin. Homemade preparations contain no preservatives. Because of this, make small batches that you can use within a week or so.

BODY CARE

SKIN CARE

The simplest and best way to care for skin, whether to soothe and heal or to refresh and stimulate, is to include herbs in your bath regimen. A leisurely soak is a good way to "de-stress," but it also helps keep skin free of dead cells, dirt, and excess oil so that sweat glands can help rid the body of waste.

As a first step to the bath, rub skin to remove the dead cells and to stimulate circulation. Use a dry body brush or loofah sponge, and brush gently but thoroughly with a circular motion. On occasion, use a salt rub.

To make a rub, combine 1 tablespoon of coarse sea salt, 1 tablespoon of herb-infused oil, and add two drops of essential oil, if desired. Lightly oil the body first, matching the oil to skin type (see page 48). Then, standing in the tub or shower, rub the salt-oil mixture onto the skin in a firm, circular motion. Bathe or shower, then apply an herbal massage oil.

Incorporate herbs into the bath with bags, infusions, salts, vinegars, or oils. Choose herbs for the bath based on skin type, as listed under facial care (see page 49), or on therapeutic need. The most widely used herbs for aching muscles and joints are sage, rosemary, or thyme, while for stress and insomnia, chamomile, lavender, or lemon balm are preferred. Other popular bath herbs include rose petals, mint, bay, lemongrass, comfrey, savory, and hyssop.

BATH BAG: Put ½ to 1 cup fresh or dried herbs into a 4- by 6-inch muslin or lace bag made specifically for the purpose, or place herbs in the center of a washcloth and secure with a ribbon or rubber band. If desired, add oatmeal or wheat bran, which are also soothing. Add the bath bag to the tub as it fills with water, then use it to scrub the body.

INFUSION: Make a strong infusion with 1 cup of fresh or ½ cup dried herbs in 4 cups water, simmering for 20 minutes and steeping for 30 minutes. Strain and add to bathwater.

More than just a pretty face in the garden, calendula blossoms can be used to soothe chapped hands, as a foot soak, and as an herbal rinse to make hair shiny.

The flowers of roses and lavender are familiar herbs with healthful benefits in herbal preparations for face and body.

BATH SALT: This softens skin and eases joint and muscle soreness. In a large bowl, thoroughly combine 2 cups Epsom salts, 1 cup baking soda, 1 cup instant dry milk, and 1 cup finely ground dried herbs. If desired, you can also add 1 teaspoon of your favorite essential oil. Store in a tightly covered, labeled glass jar. Add 2 to 4 tablespoons to bathwater.

BATH VINEGAR: This is especially good for softening skin and relieving skin irritations. Put 2 cups fresh or 1 cup dried herbs in a glass jar. Cover with 4 cups cider vinegar. Cap jar tightly with a nonmetal lid and put in a dark, cool place for three weeks. Strain and bottle. Add ½ cup to bathwater.

BATH OIL: There are two types of bath oils: floating and dispersible. For a floating oil, 2 to 3 tablespoons of an herb-infused oil are added to the bathwater and massaged into the skin. The downside is that the tub is more difficult to clean. A dispersible oil has an emulsifier to help it blend with water. To make, combine 1 cup herb-infused oil with 2 tablespoons of a coconut-based shampoo and 1 to 3 teaspoons of an essential oil. Bottle and shake before adding 1 to 2 tablespoons to bathwater.

For those who prefer to shower, use a bath bag filled with herbs or oat cleanser as your washcloth, then rub your body with an herbal massage oil or splash on herbal infusions.

Massage oils can be homemade herb-infused oils or can be made by combining a small amount of essential oil in a carrier oil, such as sweet almond or sunflower. Mix in small amounts, such as 1 teaspoon essential oil with 3 tablespoons carrier oil. Store in a dark glass bottle. Pour about 1 teaspoon into your hands, then rub gently onto the body.

HAND AND NAIL CARE

Hands tend to get neglected in day-to-day activities, and it's difficult to always wear gloves when gardening. One remedy for rough, chapped hands is an infusion of lady's mantle, fennel, calendula, comfrey, marsh mallow, or chamomile. After washing hands, dip them into the infusion for about a minute before drying with a soft cloth. Hand creams provide further care. Use any of the above herbs in one of these recipes.

HAND LOTION: Make an infusion by pouring ½ cup boiling water over 2 tablespoons fresh or 1 tablespoon dried herb. Cool and strain. Combine in a saucepan with 2 teaspoons arrowroot and 2 tablespoons glycerin. Cook over low heat until thick. Cool slightly and pour into a small jar.

HAND CREAM: Make an infusion by pouring ¼ cup boiling water over 1 tablespoon fresh or ½ tablespoon dried herb. Cool and strain. In a small saucepan over low heat, combine 2 tablespoons each cocoa or shea butter and almond oil with ½ ounce grated beeswax, stirring until melted. Stir in 1 teaspoon glycerin and the cool, strained infusion, then remove from the heat and continue stirring. When no longer hot to the touch, stir in 6 drops tincture of benzoin and continue stirring until cool. Pour into a small jar. NOTE: Tincture of benzoin acts as a preservative. You may substitute ½ teaspoon of borax dissolved in the infusion.

NAILS: To strengthen nails, soak them in a warm infusion made with dill leaves or horsetail stems.

FOOT CARE

Our feet bear us day in and day out, yet we often neglect them. Try giving them herbal footbaths and massages with an herbal oil, which will relieve aching and tiredness as it stimulates circulation.

For an herbal footbath, choose a container big enough for your feet and deep enough to cover as much of your calves as possible. Make an infusion with ½ cup fresh or ¼ cup dried herbs and 2 cups boiling water. Let steep for 30 minutes. Add the infusion to the container filled with hot water. Soak feet for 20 minutes. Among the best herbs for a footbath are rosemary, sage, thyme, mint, and pennyroyal.

To massage feet, use a hot- or cold-infused herbal oil made with linden or calendula flowers or mugwort leaves.

HAIR CARE

Healthy, shiny hair is as much due to inner health as to how the hair itself is treated. Still, the use of gentle herbal shampoos, rinses, and other products can contribute to beautiful hair.

PRE-SHAMPOO TREATMENT: Use this every other week, or weekly, if hair is particularly damaged. A simple treatment is to use 2 tablespoons of warmed herb-infused oil. Alternatively, combine one beaten egg, 1 teaspoon glycerin, and 1 tablespoon herb-infused oil. Massage treatment into hair and scalp. Then cover hair with a shower cap and wrap in a towel dampened with very hot water and wrung out well. Leave treatment on for 30 minutes. Shampoo and rinse as normal.

HERB-CASTILE SHAMPOO: Make an infusion or decoction, using one or more herbs for your hair type or condition. Mix this with liquid castile soap (available from natural-foods stores) using 1 part herb infusion to 3 parts soap.

HERBAL HAIR RINSE: In order to restore and maintain the pH balance of your hair, an acidic rinse should be used after shampooing. To make an acidic herbal hair rinse, add 1 tablespoon of vinegar to 2 cups of herbal infusion or decoction.

■ HERBS FOR NORMAL HAIR: Basil, bay, clover, comfrey root, lavender, lemon balm, nettle, rosemary, southernwood, wormwood

■ HERBS FOR DRY HAIR: Chamomile, comfrey root, elder, lavender, mallow root, orange peel

■ HERBS FOR OILY HAIR: Lemongrass, lemon peel, willow bark

■ HERBS FOR DARK HAIR: Nettle, rosemary, sage, thyme

■ HERBS FOR FAIR HAIR: Calendula, chamomile

■ HERBS FOR DANDRUFF: Comfrey root, marsh mallow root, nettle, rosemary, willow bark

■ HERBS FOR CONDITIONING: Lavender, lemongrass, nettle, rosemary, sage

■ HERBS FOR SHINY HAIR: Calendula, chamomile, nettle, rosemary, sage

Body care, of course, begins from the inside out with healthy eating. External care of skin, hands, nails, feet, and hair with herbs is a natural complement. For those who don't have time to use herbal body care every day, set aside a regular "herbal spa" day.

FRAGRANT HERBS IN THE GARDEN

Walking along a path of fragrant herbs on a warm, sunny day, with the various scents wafting around you, is a joyous testament to the wonders and benefits of their natural fragrances. Even though few people will want to go to the trouble of distilling their own essential oils from the plants in their garden, making aromatic herbs an integral part of a garden can add a whole new dimension to its charm.

Fortunately, many of the best herbs for fragrance already rank among everyone's favorites. And it's easy to tailor your herb garden to a specific effect. For example, if you want your garden to be a place of serenity and calm, the scents of chamomile, lavender, rose geranium, and sweet marjoram all have a soothing, relaxing effect. On the other hand, if you seek a place of rejuvenation, then plants such as beebalm, rosemary, or thyme would be good choices for their invigorating effects.

The fragrances of herbs have beneficial effects on our bodies and our spirits. Plant your favorite herbs near paths and benches so they can be readily enjoyed outdoors, then use them for decorative crafts year-round.

When planning an herb garden, think ahead to the ways you want to bring the fragrance indoors. If you enjoy putting together potpourris, sachets, wreaths, and bouquets, then make sure you grow the extra plants you'll need for these. Consider, too, which herb fragrances bring you the most joy. Include these throughout your yard, especially around outdoor living areas and along paths.

Then, not only will your yard bring you extra joy whenever you're outdoors, but it will also express your personality to your visitors and guests, and perhaps bring them the same joy.

USING HERBS FOR FRAGRANCE

Making fragrant crafts can be a relaxing hobby that yields beauty and scent in your home as well as for sharing with friends.

The fragrances of herbs and flowers are a powerful healing and restorative tool. Having the beloved scents of a summer's day year-round indoors brings pleasure and helps to make our homes a haven. Although the practice of aromatherapy is based on the use of essential oils, you can enjoy the beneficial effects of fragrance from the natural scents of herbs and flowers.

For thousands of years, people have employed fragrance to soothe pain, lift depression, improve sleep, and enhance passion. Over time, people have concluded that certain plant fragrances can have specific benefits. For example, lavender, clary sage, and geranium are said to encourage relaxation. The versatile lavender is also uplifting, along with the scents of rosemary, citrus, and cedar. Rose is the fragrance of romance, while peppermint, basil, eucalyptus, fir, and ginger are said to clear the mind, relieve mental fatigue and tension, and improve alertness and focus.

There are many ways—indoors and outdoors—to surround yourself with these and other beneficial fragrances.

In the garden, place aromatic plants where you'll often come into contact with them. In your home, add aromatic plants to bouquets during the summer. For fragrance indoors year-round, incorporate fragrance in every room with fresh and dried herbs.

Of course, when you cook with herbs or use them in the bath or in cosmetics, you get the benefit of fragrance. But there are other ways to make fragrances accessible, such as potpourris, sachets, sleep pillows, eye masks, wreaths, and nosegays.

USING FRAGRANT HERBS

POTPOURRI

Gently scent your home with the fragrances of potpourris made from herbs. Early potpourris were damp mixtures of rose petals, salt, and spices, hence the name, derived from the French *pourrir*, meaning "to rot." Today's potpourris are more likely to be dry mixtures of blossoms, leaves, and seeds, sometimes with a bit of essential oil for extra fragrance, plus a fixative to hold the fragrances and a gum resin to unite them.

Homemade potpourris have gentle, lingering scents. Sachets filled with potpourri can perfume linens, stationery, closets, even cars, with their fragrance.

To make your own potpourris, choose flowers and herbs that hold their scent well when dried. Lavender and rose petals are the classic flowers, but some others are orange, chamomile, heliotrope, honeysuckle, jasmine, lilac, sweet pea, and tuberose.

Among the leaves to consider are those of herbs like angelica, cinnamon basil, hyssop, mint, rosemary, and scented geranium, as well as the "lemon" herbs and evergreen needles.

Whole spices, such as allspice, cinnamon, cloves, nutmeg, and star anise, contribute an exotic undertone, while dried lemon or orange peel adds a clean, fresh note.

Sometimes colorful dried flowers or tiny hemlock cones are included in potpourris for their appearance.

When creating a potpourri, think about how the various scents will complement each other. Usually, no more than four to six different flowers or leaves, three or four spices or other ingredients, and two or three essential oils are used in potpourris.

To maintain the fresh fragrance for as long as possible, add a fixative to potpourris. The best ones are derived from plants. Orrisroot and calamus root can be grown in the garden or purchased, while oak moss is usually purchased. To prepare your own, scrub the roots of orris or calamus, dice into ¼-inch pieces, and dry thoroughly in a warm, dark, well-ventilated place. Gum resins, such as gum arabic, gum benzoin, frankincense, myrrh, and gum styrax (a fragrant balsam), act as fusing agents to pull the scents together.

Begin making potpourri by sprinkling 10 to 20 drops of essential oil over 2 to 4 tablespoons of chopped orrisroot or calamus root or 1 cup oak moss in a glass jar. Cap tightly, shake, and let sit for two days. Then, combine 4 cups dried flowers and herbs, 1 to 3 tablespoons crushed spices, and 1½ teaspoons of a powdered gum resin in a large bowl. Sprinkle on oil-fixative mixture and stir thoroughly. Pour into a large glass jar. Cap tightly. Put in a warm, dark place. Shake gently twice a week for four weeks.

SACHETS

Sachets are cloth bags filled with crushed potpourri. These are traditionally placed among bed and bath linens or in lingerie drawers and closets, but they also can be placed in boxes of writing paper, hung on hangers, the backs of chairs, or bedposts, or even placed over the vents in the car. Usually no larger than 3 or 4 inches, sachets can be made from any fabric and, if desired,

Attach a sachet to a padded hanger for a special dress.

embellished with lace or needlework.

MOTH BAGS

Keep clothes moths at bay by putting a few sachets of dried moth-repelling herbs in closets and among sweaters in chests of drawers.

The most important of these moth-repellent herbs are southernwood, wormwood, and tansy, but others often included are costmary, lavender, lemon verbena, pennyroyal, rosemary, rue, sage,

EYE MASK

Reduce stress and ease a headache by lying down and covering your eyes with a soothing eye mask filled with lavender. To make, choose a soft fabric, such as silk or velvet, and cut a 5- by 18-inch-long piece. Fold in half, right sides together, matching short ends. Stitch the two long sides. Trim corners and turn right side out. Fill with about 1 cup flax seed and ½ cup dried lavender flowers. Turn the edges of the open end inside and whipstitch shut.

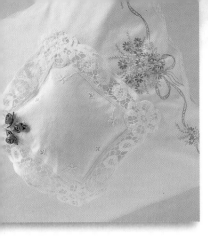

Tuck a small pillow filled with dried hops, lavender, mint, or bergamot inside the pillowcase to induce sleep and relieve stress.

santolina, sweet marjoram, sweet woodruff, and the various thymes and mints. Crushed spices, orange or lemon peel, and cedar shavings may also be added.

SLEEP PILLOWS

Because the fragrances of certain herbs are believed to have a therapeutic effect, placing 6- by 8-inch cloth bags of herbs under the bed pillow may have a beneficial effect. Hops are best at inducing sleep, while bergamot, lavender, and mints relieve stress and headaches, and lemon balm is said to keep bad dreams away.

WREATHS

Wreaths of dried herbs and flowers bring beauty and fragrance to a home, whether hanging over a mantel or on a wall, or lying flat on a table surrounding a hurricane candle shade or punch bowl.

The easiest way to construct a wreath is by using a purchased wreath base, usually straw, wire, foam, or grapevine, and covering it with dried herbs and flowers.

Before beginning a wreath, first dry a variety of herbs, including branches, stems, flowers, and seedpods.

Artemisia 'Silver King' is

Wreaths large and small are easily decorated with the fragrant dried bounty from your herb garden.

MAKING A WREATH

Using a straw base, attach a piece of 22-gauge wire for a hanger. Starting on the inside, cover the base with a background material, such as dried artemisia, by attaching 3- to 5-inch-long stems with floral pins. Work around in one direction, overlapping and covering the stems of the previous cluster, until you get back to the first cluster. Then tuck in the stems of the last one. Continue until the upper surface is covered. Add dried flowers or other plant material, either with floral pins or a hot-glue gun.

the most widely used material for the first layer of a wreath, but other varieties of the wonderfully textured, silver-gray artemisias may be used, as well as other fragrant herbs such as hyssop, rosemary, sage, or thyme. Lavender is among the most fragrant of herb flowers. Others are the blooms of the ornamental oreganos and marjorams, roses, and Sweet Annie. Colorful dried flowers like globe amaranth, statice, and yarrow can be added, as well as berries, pods, or other dried plant material.

NOSEGAYS

These round clusters of flowers and leaves, carried in the hand, make a lovely, fragrant gift. In the Victorian era, nosegays conveyed a message by the symbolic meanings of the herbs used. A sampling of those meanings is offered in the chart at right.

SYMBOLISM

Angelica: Inspiration
Basil: Good wishes
Burnet: A merry heart
Calendula: Happiness
Caraway:
    Faithfulness
Honeysuckle:
    Generosity
Ivy: Fidelity
Lavender: Devotion
Lemon balm:
    Sympathy
Marjoram: Joy
Mint: Virtue, passion
Mugwort: Happiness
Myrtle: Love, passion
Parsley: Festivity
Pinks: Fascination
Rose: Love
Rosemary:
    Remembrance
Sage: Wisdom, virtue
Thyme: Courage
Violet: Modesty

MAKING A NOSEGAY

Using either fresh or dried flowers with 4- to 6-inch-long stems, surround a central flower with other flowers and herbs. Secure the stems with a rubber band, string, or 26-gauge covered wire. Cut an X in the center of a 6-inch paper doily or use a purchased nosegay holder. Add streamers or a bow if desired.

CHOOSING HERBS

This chapter introduces you to individual herb plants. They are arranged in alphabetical order by their best-known common name. Each herb's botanical name is also given. When buying herbs, check the botanical name to be sure of getting the plant you want. To locate a plant in this book by its botanical name, consult the index.

For each herb, general information is given about its history, folklore, flavor, and general medicinal or other uses as well as its size and the appearance of the leaves and flowers. Details as to the best growing conditions as well as how to plant, propagate, care for, harvest, and preserve each herb are provided. There also is information about how to use each herb for cooking, around the home, or as a home remedy. Be aware that many of the uses originate through folklore and may not have been tested for validity and safety. You'll also learn whether the herb is an annual, perennial, or woody plant, and its tolerance of winter temperatures. The zones mentioned refer to the USDA climate zones. A map showing these zones can be found on page 93.

Whatever reason for growing herbs, whether to add beauty to your garden, enhance the flavor of food, bring fragrance to your home, or improve health and well-being, the information provided in this chapter should ensure success.

Aloe
Aloe vera

- **Zones 9–10**

Sometimes called burn plant, aloe is often kept in a pot in the kitchen for quick relief of minor burns. It is said to have been one of Cleopatra's secret beauty ingredients and continues to be a soothing, healing part of cosmetics.

DESCRIPTION: A member of the lily family, this perennial grows 12 to 24 inches tall and as wide. In California, it can grow to 4 feet. Sword-shaped, fleshy, pale green, spiny-edged leaves spotted with white. Spikes of tubular, 1-inch long, yellow to orange flowers.

IN THE GARDEN

SITE: Full sun but tolerates partial shade. Average, well-drained soil; pH 7.0. Space 1 to 2 feet apart. Containers. When used inside, keep aloe near a sunny window.

PROPAGATION: Starts easily from offshoots, which appear at the base in spring or summer; pull off and replant them separately. Can yield a dozen or more offshoots per season.

CARE: Do not overwater, which can lead to rot. Spray mealybugs with insecticidal soap (potassium salts of fatty acids). Where not hardy, grow in pots and take indoors in winter. Be careful when moving a plant from a sunny inside window to the yard in the summer; give it a day or two in the shade to adjust.

HARVEST: Pinch the tips off leaves as needed. The cut ends heal over after pieces are broken off. The brown residue can later be removed.

USES

FOR HEALTH: Split open a leaf and apply the clear gel directly to minor burns, wounds, dry skin, fungal infections, or insect bites. Add gel to shampoo for dry or itchy scalp or dandruff.

Aloe tolerates drier soil than most herbs. It heals burns and is easily grown indoors in bright light.

Angelica
Angelica archangelica

- **Zone 4**

Revered since ancient times in northern Europe, these majestic plants grow in damp meadows and along streams. The spicy-sweet, licoricelike scent and flavor is appealing in desserts and liqueurs.

DESCRIPTION: Biennial or short-lived perennial growing 4 to 8 feet tall. Celerylike leaves to 2 feet long. Large clusters of tiny, sweetly scented flowers in late spring.

Chinese angelica (*A. sinensis*, syn. *A. polymorpha*), also known as *dang gui*, is an important Chinese medicinal herb which relieves menstrual, postpartum, and menopausal conditions. Do not use when pregnant.

Another relative, *A. gigas*, is a dramatic ornamental plant with purple stems and flowers.

IN THE GARDEN

SITE: Partial shade. Humus-rich, moist, well-drained soil; pH 6.3.

PLANTING: Sow fresh seed outdoors in early autumn. Seed requires light to germinate. Self-sows. Thin to 2 feet apart. Transplant seedlings when young. Seed loses viability after three months, but keeps up to a year if stored in a refrigerator.

CARE: To prolong the life of the plants, remove flowers before they develop. Spray aphids or spider mites with insecticidal soap.

HARVEST: Leaves or stems in early summer before flowering. Ripe seeds in late summer. One-year-old roots in autumn. Preserve by drying.

USES

IN THE KITCHEN: Seeds in cakes, cookies, or liqueurs. Seeds and stems to flavor liqueurs. Crystallize green stems for decorating pastries. Leaves in green salads, soups, or stews, or with acidic fruit, such as rhubarb, to reduce sugar needed for flavoring. Roots in breads, cakes, muffins, cookies, or liqueurs.

IN THE HOME: Dried seed heads in arrangements. Burn seeds as incense. Dried leaves in potpourri.

FOR HEALTH: Leaf infusion internally for tension, headaches, indigestion, poor blood circulation, coughs, or colds; externally in baths for sore muscles or in ointment for wounds or skin rashes. Root decoction for coughs or sore throats.

CAUTION: Do *not* use medicinally when pregnant.

Adding leaves and stems of angelica to rhubarb pie reduces the amount of sugar needed.

Anise
Pimpinella anisum
- Half-hardy Annual

Anise needs a long summer for the seeds to develop, but the foliage has a flavor similar to the seeds.

Anise adds a licorice flavor to a variety of baked goods.

DESCRIPTION: Annual, growing to 2 feet tall and 1 to 2 feet wide. Lower leaves rounded to toothed and upper leaves finely divided. Flat clusters of creamy white flowers in summer. Oval seeds ⅛ inch long.

IN THE GARDEN

SITE: Full sun. Average, well-drained soil; pH 6.0. Space 1 foot apart. Containers.

PLANTING: Sow seed directly into the garden in late spring.

CARE: May need staking or protection from wind.

HARVEST: Leaves throughout the growing season. Flowers as they open. Ripe seeds as they begin to turn gray-green. Preserve by drying.

USES

IN THE KITCHEN: Whole, crushed, or ground seed in baked goods, apple dishes, pickles, curries, eggs, soups, stews, and liqueurs. Flowers, leaves in fruit salads.

IN THE HOME: Seed in potpourri. Leaves or seed in dog pillows.

FOR HEALTH: Chew toasted seed to freshen breath and aid digestion. Seed infusion for colds, coughs, indigestion, or nausea, colic, and to stimulate milk in nursing mothers.

Anise Hyssop
Agastache foeniculum
- Zone 4

Cut off the faded flowers of anise hyssop to prevent seeds scattering around the garden.

Anise hyssop was used as a sweetener and medicine by the Native Americans of the Great Plains. The flavor hints of both anise and mint.

DESCRIPTION: Perennial, growing to 3 feet tall and 1 foot wide. Oval, anise-scented leaves. Blue flowers in late summer and autumn.

IN THE GARDEN

SITE: Full sun but tolerates partial shade. Fertile, well-drained soil; Space 1 foot apart. Containers.

PROPAGATION: Seed sown indoors in early spring. Self-sows. Cuttings in spring or summer. Division, every few years

HARVEST: Leaves as needed. Flowers when three-quarters open. Preserve by drying.

OTHER: Attracts butterflies and bees. Repels cabbage moth.

USES

IN THE KITCHEN: Leaves or flowers with fresh or baked fruit, cakes, cookies, teas, squash, sweet potatoes, carrots, sweet-and-sour pork, chicken, fish, or rice.

IN THE HOME: Leaves or flowers in potpourris. Dried flowers in wreaths. Fresh flowers in bouquets.

FOR HEALTH: Leaf infusion for poor appetite, indigestion, nausea, or feverish chills.

Arnica
Arnica montana
- Zone 2

The diminutive flowers of the alpine-growing arnica help to heal wounds and bruises.

Native to the alpine pastures of Europe, arnica has been a popular remedy for bruises and sprains since the sixteenth century. Purchase nursery-propagated plants because it is a protected species.

DESCRIPTION: Perennial, growing 1 to 2 feet tall and 6 inches wide. Oval, pointed, light green, hairy leaves to 5 inches long. Yellow, daisylike, 3-inch flowers in summer.

The North American species, *A. chamissonis*, is similar in both appearance and properties.

IN THE GARDEN

SITE: Full sun. Humus-rich, sandy, well-drained soil; pH 4.0. Space plants 8 to 12 inches apart.

PROPAGATION: Sow seed outdoors in autumn; germination may take up to two years. Division or cuttings in spring.

CARE: Grows best in areas with cool summers. Protect plants from slugs.

HARVEST: Flowers just as they become fully open. Preserve them by drying.

USES

FOR HEALTH: Flower tincture, oil, or ointment for sprains, bruises, or muscle pain. External use may cause a skin rash.

CAUTION: Do not take this herb internally or apply it to broken skin. Dermatitis may occur.

Artemisia

Artemisia species

■ **Zones 4–6**

Pungently aromatic, usually with velvety silver-gray leaves, the artemisias are among the most ancient plants used for their herbal properties. Some think the name is derived from Artemis, Greek goddess of the hunt and moon, while others point to Artemisia, a botanist 350 Years Before Christ. Among the most bitter of herbs, artemisias have been used to ward off diseases, repel insects as well as evil, cure baldness, soothe sore feet, and flavor the hallucinogenic nineteenth-century drink, absinthe. Today, their use is limited to moth repellents and herb crafts, but ornamentally it is among the most favored of herbs for the garden.

SOUTHERNWOOD, also known as lad's love or old man (*A. abrotanum*). Perennial, growing 3 to 5 feet tall and 2 feet wide. Upright, branching stems with silver-gray divided leaves. Sprays of insignificant yellow flowers in summer; zone 6.

WORMWOOD (*A. absinthium*). Perennial 2 to 4 feet tall and wide. Upright, well-branched growth with finely divided, gray-green, semi-evergreen, lemon-scented leaves. Sprays of insignificant yellow flowers in summer; zone 4. 'Lambrook

Silver' is a cultivar, and 'Powis Castle' is a 2- to 3-foot hybrid between *A. absinthium* and *A. arborescens*; both hardy to zone 6.

'SILVER KING', 'SILVER QUEEN', AND 'VALERIE FINNIS' (cultivars of *A. ludoviciana*). Perennials growing 2 to 3 feet tall and as wide. Upright stems with narrow, pointed, silvery leaves to 4 inches long. Popular for wreaths and dried arrangements; zone 5.

SWEET ANNIE (*A. annua*). Annual to 5 feet tall and 3 feet wide. Widely used in wreaths and crafts.

OTHERS: Some other perennial artemisias with a heritage of herbal uses include: Roman wormwood (*A. pontica*), with feathery silver foliage on 2- to 3-foot plants; zone 5. White mugwort (*A. lactiflora*) with deeply cut, medium green leaves to 6 inches long on 5-foot plants and showy sprays of creamy white flowers in summer; zone 5. Mugwort (*A. vulgaris*) with dark green leaves on upright, red-purple stems to 5 feet tall; zone 4.

IN THE GARDEN

SITE: Full sun. Average, well-drained soil; pH 6.6. Space plants 2 to 4 feet apart. Containers.

PROPAGATION: Difficult from seed. Divide in spring or fall, at least every four years. Cuttings in summer.

CARE: Trim new growth in spring to shape plants. Cut back to 6 inches in autumn. Dig out wandering roots to curb invasive tendency. Spray aphids with insecticidal soap.

HARVEST: Leaves as needed. Preserve by drying.

USES

IN THE HOME: Dried wormwood or southernwood leaves as moth repellents. Dried branches of any artimisia in wreaths, swags, or other herb crafts. Fresh sprigs in bouquets.

FOR HEALTH: Leaf infusion of southernwood in hair rinses.

Wormwood and other artemisias are indispensable for herbal crafts and moth repellents.

Astragalus

Astragalus membranaceus

■ **Zone 5**

Also known as huang qi or milk vetch, the roots of this herb have been an important part of traditional Chinese medicine for thousands of years. With uses ranging from allergies to a tonic for low energy and poor circulation, no wonder it's so highly thought of. Because of its wide-ranging uses, many consider it to be in the same category as the more well-known herb, ginseng. Some herbalists credit it with stimulating the immune system.

DESCRIPTION: Perennial, growing 12 to 18 inches tall and as wide. Leaves divided into 12 to 18 pairs of

leaflets. Stalks of yellow, pealike flowers in early summer.

IN THE GARDEN

SITE: Full sun. Sandy, well-drained soil; pH 7.0. Containers.

PROPAGATION: Seed sown outdoors in spring or autumn.

HARVEST: Four-year-old roots in autumn for use in decoctions, powders, and tinctures.

USES

FOR HEALTH: Root decoction to increase energy and immune resistance, prevent colds, and improve blood circulation.

CAUTION: Do not take if suffering from skin disorders.

In traditional Chinese medicine, astragalus competes with the better-known herb, ginseng.

Basil

Ocimum species and cultivars

■ **Tender Annual**

A culinary herb, beloved for its warm, spicy flavor and intoxicating scent, basil, in all its species and forms, is native to Africa, Asia, the Middle East, the Caribbean, and South America. Used for more than 2,000 years, basil was originally revered for its sanctity and spiritual powers, then was connected briefly with evil in sixteenth century Europe. The Italians never lost sight of its role in the kitchen, starting with Virgil, who is considered the first writer to mention pesto.

Ocimum basilicum is the main species for cooking, but it is highly variable, with dozens of cultivated varieties in a wide range of leaf sizes, colors, and flavors. Often, varieties with different names are similar, and, conversely, varieties with the same name from different sources may be quite different.

Varieties with a traditional basil flavor that grow about 2 feet tall and have smooth leaves to 3 inches long include 'Genoa Green Improved', 'Genoa Profumatissima', and the generically labeled 'Sweet Basil'.

Varieties with a traditional basil flavor with smooth or crinkled leaves up to 6 inches long are referred to as "lettuce-leaf basils," and may be labeled as such or as 'Napoletano', 'Mammoth', or

Synonymous with pesto, basil—with its spicy flavor—is perfect in tomato dishes as well as in desserts.

'Valentino'. 'Green Ruffles' has exceptionally puckered leaves.

Varieties growing to a rounded shape 1 foot tall with leaves to 1 inch long include 'Dwarf Bush', 'Dwarf Bush Fine Leaf', 'Bush Green', 'Miniature', 'Dwarf Italian', 'Dwarf Bouquet', 'Green Bouquet', and 'Green Globe'. 'Spicy Globe' and 'Spicy Bush' are similar but with a very strong spicy aroma and flavor. Taller plants with tiny leaves include *O. americanum* 'Sweet Fine', growing to 3 feet tall, 'Piccolo', growing to 2 feet tall, and 'Miniature Puerto Rican', growing to 20 inches tall.

Some varieties of *O. basilicum* have purplish-red leaves. These include 'Dark Opal', 'Red Rubin', 'Osmin', 'Purple Ruffles', 'Well-Sweep Miniature Purple', 'New Guinea', and 'Purple Thai', plus the purple-and-green variegated 'Holly's Painted'. Besides their ornamental value, red-leaf basils often are used to color vinegar.

Several varieties of *O. basilicum* grow in a narrow, columnar shape, reaching 2 to 4 feet tall. These include the 2-foot 'Cuban' and the taller 'Lesbos', 'Aussie Sweetie', and 'Greek Column'.

Of distinctly flavored basils, 'Anise', 'Licorice', 'Thai', 'True Thai', and 'Siam Queen' are all variations on the anise theme. Other-flavored basils include 'Spice', 'Mexican Spice', 'Cinnamon', 'Karamanos', and 'Puerto Rican'. Basils with a flavor and aroma of citrus include 'Lemon', 'Maenglak Thai', 'Mrs. Burns' Famous Lemon', 'Sweet Dani', and 'Lime'.

O. gratissimum, commonly called East Indian basil, tree basil, or fever plant, grows 4 to 6 feet tall and as wide, with pungently scented leaves to 7 inches long. It is mainly used as a medicinal herb, an insect repellent, or as an ornamental. Varieties include 'Clove', 'East Indian', 'Green', and 'West African'.

O. kilmandscharicum, or camphor basil, grows to 3 feet tall with leaves

to 3 inches long. 'African Blue' is a hybrid between this species and 'Dark Opal' with purplish leaves fading to deep green. Use both as ornamentals.

O. tenuiflorum (previously *O. sanctum*), commonly called holy or tulsi basil, is sacred to Hindus in its native India. With a scent that combines mint, camphor, clove, and cinnamon, it is said to have medicinal uses. A variety called 'Sacred' is quite different, with a citrus and spice flavor and aroma.

IN THE GARDEN

SITE: Full sun. Humus-rich, moist, well-drained soil; pH 6.0. Space 12 to 18 inches apart. Containers.

PROPAGATION: Seed sown indoors in early spring or outdoors when all danger of frost is past.

CARE: Grows best in areas with hot summers. Remove flowers by cutting about one-fourth of stem just above first set of leaves to encourage branching and more leaves. Spray aphids or whiteflies with horticultural soap. Protect from slugs. Smaller-leaved types are the easiest to grow indoors.

HARVEST: Leaves as needed. Flowers as they open. Preserve by chopping, mixing with oil, and freezing; much of the flavor is lost in drying.

USES

IN THE KITCHEN: Leaves in vinegars, pestos, lamb, fish, poultry, beans, pastas, rice, tomato sauces, cheeses, eggs, salads, vegetables, soups, stews, fruit desserts, cookies, breads, or muffins. Flowers in salads or as garnish.

IN THE HOME: Repels flies and mosquitoes around decks, patios, and doorways, especially *O. gratissimum* and *O. tenuiflorum*. Add leaves of spice- or lemon-scented varieties to potpourris.

FOR HEALTH: All types as a leaf infusion internally for headaches, fevers, colds, indigestion, nausea, constipation, anxiety, or exhaustion; externally in bath to invigorate or in hair rinse for shine. Splash leaf infusion on body to help repel mosquitoes. Seed poultice for wounds.

Bay
Laurus nobilis

■ Zone 8

Bay is an ancient herb from southern Europe, where it was considered sacred to the Greek god Apollo. It was thought to guard against disease, and it crowned poets and athletes in Rome. Today, the warm, aromatic flavor and scent are considered essential in cooking.

DESCRIPTION: Woody evergreen shrub or tree, growing to 50 feet tall. Leathery, oval, dark green leaves. Small, creamy yellow flowers in spring. Dark purple berries.

The cultivar 'Angustifolia' has wavy-edged leaves and 'Aurea' has yellow-tinged leaves.

IN THE GARDEN

SITE: Full sun to partial shade. Humus-rich, well-drained soil; pH 6.6. Containers.

PROPAGATION: Seed difficult. Cuttings in autumn. Layering in spring. Cutting and layering require many months to develop roots.

CARE: Where not hardy, grow in pots and bring indoors in winter. Can be trained as a standard or topiary. Fertilize in spring. Highly susceptible to scale; spray with a summer horticultural oil (a light oil that deters insects) or wipe with a cotton swab dipped in alcohol. Protect from wind.

HARVEST: Leaves as needed. Preserve by drying, preferably in a flower press to keep them flat.

USES

IN THE KITCHEN: Leaves in soups, stews, stocks, marinades, tomato sauces, pickles, shellfish boils, beans, grains, long-cooked meat dishes, custard desserts, or on coals when grilling. Remove bay leaf from food before serving.

IN THE HOME: Wreaths or potpourris. In flour, rice, grains, or dried figs to deter weevils.

FOR HEALTH: Leaf infusion internally for indigestion, poor appetite, or flatulence; externally in bathwater for muscle ache or joint pain, hair rinse for dandruff, skin tonic, or compress for sore joints, sprains, or bruises.

CAUTION: Never take essential oil internally; may also cause dermatitis.

For bay to develop bushy and compact when grown in a container, regularly pinch out stem tips.

Bergamot
Monarda didyma

■ Zone 4

Bergamot, also known as beebalm, is a North American native that is widely grown as an ornamental flower and as an herb. The Oswego Indians drank a tea of the leaves for colds and sore throats and introduced it to early settlers, who used it as a tea substitute after the Boston Tea Party. The common name is derived from the resemblance of the scent to Italian bergamot oranges.

DESCRIPTION: Perennial, growing 3 to 4 feet tall. Oval, pointed, slightly hairy, dark green leaves with a minty citrus scent and flavor. Clusters of tubular, two-lipped, edible scarlet flowers; cultivars available in shades of scarlet, magenta, purple, pink, or white.

Two other perennial monardas are wild monarda (*M. fistulosa*), with white to lavender flowers (zone 3), and horsemint (*M. punctata*), with purple-spotted yellow flowers (zone 5).

Lemon mint (*M. citriodora*) is an annual or biennial growing to 2 feet tall with white to pink flowers and lemon-scented leaves.

IN THE GARDEN

SITE: Full sun to partial shade. Humus-rich, moist, well-drained soil. Space 2 feet apart. Containers.

PROPAGATION: Variable from seed. Division in spring, preferably every three years. Cuttings in early summer.

CARE: Control powdery mildew with good air circulation and by cutting plants back to the ground after flowering, or grow mildew-resistant varieties, including 'Marshall's Delight', 'Petite Delight', and 'Petite Wonder'.

HARVEST: Leaves as needed. Flowers as soon as fully open. Preserve by drying.

OTHER: Attracts bumblebees, hummingbirds, and butterflies.

USES

IN THE KITCHEN: Flowers or leaves in fruit or green salads, teas, flavoring for black tea, wines, lemonade, pork, duck, goose, sausages, or jellies.

IN THE HOME: Leaves or flowers in potpourri. Dried flowers in crafts. Fresh flowers in bouquets.

FOR HEALTH: Leaf infusion has been used internally for colds, fevers, indigestion, nausea, flatulence, insomnia, or menstrual pain; externally in bath or in poultice for painful joints. Horsemint is considered to be stronger medicinally and is sometimes used for skin problems.

The unusual flowers of bergamot have nectar scented with the smell of oranges.

Black Cohosh
Cimicifuga racemosa

■ **Zone 3**

Originating in the northeastern United States, black cohosh was a Native American remedy for a variety of ills, including "women's problems," hence another common name, squawroot. Besides its medicinal applications today, black cohosh is an outstanding ornamental for the shady flower border or in a natural, woodland setting.

Black cohosh is an ornamental perennial herb for the shade garden. The roots have medicinal properties.

DESCRIPTION: Long-lived perennial, growing to 6 feet tall and 3 feet wide. Dark green, palmately divided, toothed leaves. Bottlebrush spires, to 2 feet, of small, fragrant, white flowers which bloom from mid- to late summer.

Foetid bugbane (*C. foetida*) is an Asian species with a similar appearance and properties, which is a popular and traditional Chinese medicine; zone 4.

IN THE GARDEN

SITE: Partial shade. Deep, humus-rich, moist, well-drained soil; pH 6.0. Space 3 feet apart.
PROPAGATION: Seed sown outdoors in autumn. Division in spring or autumn.
CARE: Takes several years to become established.
HARVEST: Roots in autumn. Preserve by drying.

USES

FOR THE HOME: Fresh or dried flowers or the seed spikes in bouquets.
FOR HEALTH: Root decoction or tincture traditionally used internally for muscle or joint pain, headaches, arthritis, menstrual cramps, coughs, fevers, high blood pressure, or tinnitus. Reduces progesterone levels in women.
CAUTION: Women who are or who could be pregnant or are breast-feeding should *not* use this herb.

Borage
Borago officinalis

■ **Hardy Annual**

Can borage actually make people happy, dispel melancholy, or give courage? Folklore notwithstanding, the traits may come from borage's high potassium content and its stimulating effect on the adrenal glands. No doubt, too, that the cucumber-flavored leaves and small, starry flowers simply bring pleasure.

DESCRIPTION: Hardy annual, growing to 2 feet tall and as wide. Hollow, bristly, sprawling stems and bristly oval leaves up to 6 inches long. Star-shaped, 1-inch flowers, which start out pink and mature to blue and bloom throughout summer. 'Alba' is a white-flowered cultivar.

Folklore has it that, as a companion plant, borage repels Japanese beetles and tomato hornworms.

IN THE GARDEN

SITE: Full sun but tolerates partial shade. Humus-rich, sandy, moist, well-drained soil; pH 6.6. Space 2 feet apart. Containers.
PROPAGATION: Seed sown outdoors in late spring. Self-sows. Does not transplant well, except when very young.
CARE: Remove faded flowers to prolong flowering. Spray aphids with insecticidal soap. Grows best in cool weather.
HARVEST: Leaves when young. Flowers just as they are fully open. Preserve by drying.

OTHER: Improves insect or disease resistance in nearby plants. Companion plant to strawberries. Attracts bees.

USES

IN THE KITCHEN: Flowers in punch, iced drinks, ice cubes, green or fruit salads, vinegars, or over sliced tomatoes. Crystallize flowers for decorating pastries. Leaves in soups, cooked greens, salads, butters, cheese or yogurt dips, tea sandwiches, fish, poultry, eggs, teas, punches, sorbets, vinegars, or salt-free herb-seasoning blends. Combines well with dill, mint, and garlic.
IN THE HOME: Dried flowers in potpourris. Fresh flowers in bouquets.
FOR HEALTH: Leaf infusion internally for colds, coughs, fevers, insomnia, or nervous tension. Leaves in face packs for dry skin, in baths, or in a poultice for bruises or irritated skin. Seeds are high in gamma-linoleic acid.

Calendula
Calendula officinalis
- **Annual**

Calendula has been commonly called marybud, bull's-eye, holligold, poor man's saffron, and pot marigold. It was valued in ancient Greek, Roman, Persian, Egyptian, and Indian cultures. Later, it was widely used in Europe and England, especially in cooking and for its purported magical properties. Calendula brings bright, cheery flowers to the garden, color and peppery flavor to food, and a soothing, healing antiseptic to skin.

DESCRIPTION: Annual, growing 8 to 24 inches tall, depending on the variety. Oval, pointed leaves to 3 inches long on angular stems. Daisylike flowers in summer, 2 to 4 inches across in shades of yellow, gold, apricot, or orange. The best varieties for herbal use are those with large petals, such as 'Pacific Beauty', 'Indian Prince', or 'Sunglow'.

IN THE GARDEN

SITE: Full sun but tolerates partial shade in hot climates. Average, well-drained soil; pH 6.6. Space 8 to 12 inches apart. Containers.

PROPAGATION: Seed sown indoors in early spring or directly outdoors two weeks before last frost. Self-sows.

CARE: Grows best in climates with cool summers or in spring and autumn in hotter climates. Deadhead to prolong flowering. Control slugs with barriers or traps. Spray aphids with insecticidal soap. Remove mildewed leaves.

HARVEST: Leaves when young. Flowers as they open, using the petals. Preserve by drying.

USES

IN THE KITCHEN: Petals in salads, with greens, in soups, stews, sandwiches, cheeses, eggs, butters, grains, rice, dumplings, cakes, cookies, puddings, vinegars, liqueurs, or wines.

IN THE HOME: Petals in potpourri. Fresh flowers in bouquets.

FOR HEALTH: Petal infusion or tincture internally for indigestion, eczema, or menstrual pain; externally in facial tonic for large pores, acne, mouthwash for infected gums, bathwater to heal and soften skin, hair rinse for oily hair, compresses for wounds, burns, or stings. Petal oil or ointment for skin rashes, athlete's foot, varicose veins, bruises, or minor cuts or burns.

'Pacific Beauty' calendula has large petals that can substitute for the more expensive saffron.

Caraway
Carum carvi
- **Zone 4**

Caraway has been a flavoring and medicine for more than 5,000 years. Its folklore properties included keeping lovers and poultry close to home. The common name is derived from the ancient Arabic word for seed, *karawya*.

DESCRIPTION: Biennial, growing to 2 feet tall and as wide. Finely cut, feathery leaves on floppy stems. Flat heads of tiny white flowers in midsummer. Ridged, brown, ¼-inch-long, crescent-shaped seeds.

IN THE GARDEN

SITE: Full sun. Deeply tilled, average, well-drained soil. Space 8 inches apart. Containers.

PROPAGATION: Seed sown directly in the soil outdoors in spring or autumn. Best germination in autumn with fresh seed.

CARE: Mulch plants in winter.

HARVEST: Young leaves as needed. Seed heads as they turn brown; preserve by drying. Roots in autumn after seed harvest.

USES

IN THE KITCHEN: Seeds in breads, cakes, cookies, soups, sauces, stews, pork, beef, goose, vegetables, pickled vegetables, sauerkraut, cheeses, eggs, grains, apples, or liqueurs. Candy the seeds. Young leaves in fruit or green salads, herb cheeses, or butters. Roots eaten as a vegetable.

IN THE HOME: Seeds in cooked cabbage help reduce odor.

FOR HEALTH: Seed eaten raw or in infusion before meals to increase appetite or after meals to aid digestion, sweeten breath, or relieve flatulence; also for menstrual cramps or coughs.

CAUTION: Do not take essential oil of caraway internally.

Caraway seeds not only flavor foods, but when cooked with cabbage, they reduce the disagreeable odor.

Catnip

Nepeta cataria

- **Zone 4**

Catnip's common name is no surprise to anyone who has seen the pleasure that cats take in rolling in it. The genus name may be derived from the Roman town of Nepeti, where, according to folklore, catnip grew profusely. Catnip is also a seasoning and medicinal herb.

Catnip isn't just for cats. Add the young leaves or flowers to salads or make a soothing cup of hot tea.

DESCRIPTION: Perennial, growing to 3 feet tall and 2 feet wide. Sprawling stems with triangular, toothed, 2-inch-long leaves smelling of camphor, thyme, and pennyroyal. Leaves and stems covered with downy white fuzz. Small, tubular, white to pink, edible flowers in summer. The cultivar 'Citriodora' has a lemon scent and flavor.

Several other *Nepeta* species are good ornamental flowers but with a much milder scent and less appeal to cats. Among the best of these are *N.* × *faassenii* and *N.* 'Six Hills Giant', and *N.* × *faassenii* 'Walker's Low'.

IN THE GARDEN

SITE: Full sun to partial shade. Average, well-drained soil; pH 6.6. Good winter drainage is essential. Space 12 to 18 inches apart. Containers.

PROPAGATION: Seed sown directly into the garden in spring or autumn. Self-sows. Division in spring. Cuttings in spring.

CARE: Protect plants from cats until well-established. When the first flowering is finished, cut back to several inches to get a second blooming and to maintain shape.

HARVEST: Leaves when young for eating. Leaves and flowers when in full bloom for medicinal use. Preserve by drying.

OTHER: Planting it near vegetables is said to deter flea beetles, aphids, and beetles.

USES

IN THE KITCHEN: Young leaves in green salads or tea. Add leaves to stews or rub meat with them before roasting.

IN THE HOME: Stuff cloth "mice" with dried leaves as toys for cats. Flowers in bouquets.

FOR HEALTH: Infusion of leaves internally to relieve colds, flu, fevers, insomnia, nervous tension, indigestion, flatulence, or diarrhea; externally to relieve scalp irritations. Poultice of leaves and flowers for bruises. Colic in babies.

Cayenne

Capsicum annuum

- **Annual**

Native to the tropical regions of the Americas, cayenne and other hot peppers were reintroduced to the West in the sixteenth century. Since then, they have insinuated

Hot peppers spice up food around the world, and they also help relieve arthritis, sore throat, and indigestion.

themselves into far-flung cuisines with their hot, burning taste. Medicinally, they are a warming stimulant, improving blood circulation and digestion, plus relieving joint pain. Many are considered attractive ornamentals when fruiting, and there are a number of dwarf cultivars suitable for growing in containers.

DESCRIPTION: Tender annual, growing 1 to 3 feet tall, depending on the cultivar. Oval, pointed leaves 1 to 4 inches long. White, ½-inch flowers throughout summer. Fruit ripens in shades of red, orange, or yellow, from summer to fall.

IN THE GARDEN

SITE: Full sun. Humus-rich, moist, well-drained soil; pH 6.8. Plant 18 inches to 2 feet apart. Containers.

PROPAGATION: Seed sown indoors in early spring.

HARVEST: Fruit when ripe. Cut from the plant leaving ½ inch of stem. Preserve by drying. The whole plant can be pulled up before frost and hung upside down until the peppers dry.

USES

IN THE KITCHEN: Remove seeds and veins and discard. In salsa, barbecue, soups, stews, cheeses, eggs, sauces, curries, or Mexican or Southeast Asian dishes.

IN THE HOME: Wreaths.

FOR HEALTH: Infused oil or ointment externally for sore joints or poor circulation. Powdered or crushed with lemon juice, hot water, and honey for sore throat gargle. Tincture for arthritis or indigestion.

CAUTION: Handle carefully, being especially careful around eyes or broken skin. Do not take medicinally when pregnant or breast-feeding.

Chamomile

Chamaemelum nobile

■ **Zone 4**

Peter Rabbit's mother wasn't the first to recommend a tea made from chamomile flowers, as they were revered by ancient Egyptians and Anglo-Saxons for their healing qualities. Another common name is Roman chamomile.

DESCRIPTION: Perennial, growing to 8 inches tall and 18 inches wide. Finely cut, feathery leaves. Daisylike, 1-inch flowers in late summer and autumn. 'Flore Pleno' has double flowers. 'Treneague' is a nonflowering, mat-forming plant growing 1 inch tall, and is best for chamomile lawns.

A similar plant is German chamomile, *Matricaria recutita*, an annual that grows to 24 inches tall and 6 inches wide. The leaves have a lighter scent and less bitter taste, but a slightly higher proportion of the volatile oil that acts as an anti-inflammatory and analgesic.

IN THE GARDEN

SITE: Full sun but tolerates partial shade. Sandy, average, well-drained soil; pH 7.0. Space Roman chamomile 18 inches apart and German chamomile 6 inches apart. Containers.

PROPAGATION: Sow Roman or German chamomile seed directly into the garden in spring or autumn. Divide cultivars in early spring; cultivars must be divided as they do not produce seed.

HARVEST: Leaves as needed. Flowers the day they open. Preserve by drying; keep for only one year.

OTHER: Flower infusion prevents damping-off in seedlings and speeds compost decomposition.

USES

IN THE HOME: Infusion to prolong the life of cut flowers. Flowers and leaves in potpourris.

FOR HEALTH: Infusion of flowers used internally for indigestion, nausea, fever, insomnia, hay fever, hyperactivity, or menstrual cramps; externally as a rinse for blonde hair or dandruff, facial tonic, lotion, cream, or steam, hand soak, eye compress, or in bath. Use as an ointment or oil for wounds, sunburn, eczema, or itchy skin.

CAUTION: People allergic to ragweed may react to chamomile. Handling it may cause dermatitis. Drink the tea sparingly, no more than ½ cup daily for no more than two weeks at a time.

A cheery plant in the garden, chamomile yields flowers that are a traditional stomachache remedy.

Chervil

Anthriscus cerefolium

■ **Hardy Annual**

The sweet aroma and refreshing flavor of chervil complements a wide range of foods, and it is essential in French cooking. Grown since ancient Roman times, chervil was part of medicinal spring tonics because it is rich in vitamin C, beta carotene, iron, and magnesium.

DESCRIPTION: Hardy cool-season annual, growing 12 to 18 inches tall. Fine-textured, fernlike leaves. Clusters of tiny white flowers in early summer. The cultivar 'Crispum' has curly leaves.

IN THE GARDEN

SITE: Partial shade. Humus-rich, moist, well-drained soil; pH 6.5. Space 6 inches apart. Containers.

PROPAGATION: Seed sown directly into the garden at two-week intervals from early spring until summer, then again in late summer to early autumn. Needs light to germinate. Self-sows.

CARE: Best in cool, moist weather; goes to seed quickly with high temperatures and dry soil. Pinch out flower stalks to prolong growth. For fresh leaves year-round, overwinter in a cold frame or grow indoors.

HARVEST: Leaves as needed until flowering. Preserve by freezing.

OTHER: Is said to repel slugs and keeps ants and aphids away from lettuce.

USES

IN THE KITCHEN: Leaves in salads, vegetables, chicken, fish, eggs, soups, sauces, vinegars, or butters. Add near the end of cooking.

IN THE HOME: Leaves or flowers in potpourris. Fresh flowers in bouquets or nosegays.

FOR HEALTH: Leaf infusion taken internally is said to aid digestion and improve liver and kidney functions and circulation; externally in facial cleansers or in tonics or in compresses for sore joints, eczema, or wounds.

Chervil flourishes in cool weather, and its leaves impart a delicate flavor of anise to many French dishes.

Chives

Allium schoenoprasum

■ **Zone 3**

Native to North America, Europe, and Asia, chives were not used in the West until Marco Polo brought them from China, where they've been a favorite for 5,000 years. With a delicate onion flavor, chives enhance a number of foods. They

With grassy leaves and pink flowers, chives are an ornamental as well as a delicious herb.

blend especially well with shallots, marjoram, and tarragon.

DESCRIPTION: Perennial, growing to 12 to 18 inches tall, forming clumps 12 to 18 inches across. Slender, hollow leaves. Globular, 1-inch heads of purplish-pink flowers in early summer. The cultivar 'Forescate' grows somewhat larger and with pinker flowers; 'Grolau' is a good variety for indoors; 'Profusion' blooms for a long period and is also good indoors. Dwarf and white-flowered forms also available.

Garlic or Chinese chives (*A. tuberosum*) have flat, solid leaves with a mild garlic flavor and 2-inch heads of white flowers. Hardy to zone 3. Mauve-flowered form.

IN THE GARDEN

SITE: Full sun. Humus-rich, well-drained soil; pH 6.0. Space about 6 inches apart.

PROPAGATION: Seed sown indoors in early spring. Division in early spring or autumn in clumps of six bulbs; best done every three years to prevent crowding. Garlic chives readily self-sow.

CARE: Cut plants back to 2 inches after flowering to encourage new, tender leaf growth; trim regularly where it grows year-round. For an indoor winter crop, start seeds in early autumn or dig a small clump, pot up, and leave outside until the soil freezes, then bring indoors.

HARVEST: Leaves as needed, cutting at the base. Flowers just as they open. Preserve by freezing.

OTHER: Leaf infusion as a spray for aphids or mildew. In mixed plantings, helps to repel insects.

USES

IN THE KITCHEN: Leaves or flowers in salads, vegetables, poultry, fish, soups, sauces, eggs, cheeses, butters, or vinegars. Add at the end of cooking or use as a garnish.

IN THE HOME: Fresh flowers in bouquets. Dried flowers in wreaths and other herbal crafts.

FOR HEALTH: Leaves stimulate appetite and improve digestion.

Cilantro, Coriander

Coriandrum sativum

■ **Hardy Annual**

Whether referred to as cilantro or coriander, this is one of the most widely used herbs. The spicy, citrus-flavored seeds, called coriander, were compared in the Bible to

Because cilantro leaves are best when young, make new plantings in summer for a continuous supply.

manna. The leaves, referred to as cilantro, have a pungent aroma that is either loved or hated.

DESCRIPTION: Hardy annual, growing to 2 feet tall. Small, open clusters of tiny pinkish white flowers in early to midsummer. Rounded, ribbed, beige seeds. 'Chinese', 'Slow-Bolt', and 'Long Standing' are said to produce leaves longer than the species.

Two other plants have leaves with a flavor similar to cilantro. Vietnamese coriander (*Polygonum odoratum*), perennial from Southeast Asia, growing 12 inches tall, with oval, pointed, 2-inch leaves, withstands hot weather and grows well indoors; zone 9. Mexican coriander (*Eryngium foetidum*), evergreen perennial, grows to 18 inches tall and wide; zone 8.

IN THE GARDEN

SITE: Full sun to partial shade. Humus-rich, moist, well-drained soil; pH 6.6. Space 6 inches apart. Containers.

PROPAGATION: Seed sown directly into the garden after last frost and monthly plantings until late summer. Transplanting may cause plants to bolt.

HARVEST: Lower leaves as needed. Seed heads when brown and orange scented. Roots as the plants die down.

USES

IN THE KITCHEN: Fresh leaves in salads, salsas, marinades, stir-fries, rice, pastas, vinegars, and with shellfish dishes. Whole or ground seeds in beans, curries, marinades, salad dressings, eggs, cheeses, lamb, sausages, pickles, chutneys, cooked fruits, breads, cakes, cookies, or coffees. Roots as a vegetable.

IN THE HOME: Seed in potpourris.

FOR HEALTH: Fresh leaves, seeds, or infusion internally before meals to stimulate appetite or after meals for indigestion, flatulence, or bad breath. Crushed seeds externally in a poultice or infused oil for sore joints or hemorrhoids.

Comfrey

Symphytum officinale

■ **Zone 5**

Comfrey was long considered a panacea for many ills, including healing broken bones. Today, we know the leaves contain alkaloids that cause liver damage and tumors, so comfrey is not ingested. Externally, it is still important in healing preparations.

DESCRIPTION: Perennial growing 2 to 4 feet tall. Hairy, rough-textured, pointed leaves to 10 inches long. Spikes of purple to white, ½-inch, bell-like flowers in late spring. Spreads rapidly and invasively.

Variegated Russian comfrey (*Symphytum × uplandicum* 'Variegatum')is grown as an ornamental perennial; zone 5.

IN THE GARDEN

SITE: Full sun to partial shade. Humus-rich, moist soil; pH 7.0. Space plants about 3 feet apart. Containers.

PROPAGATION: Germination is slow and erratic. Division in autumn, cuttings in summer and fall.

CARE: Plant in an area where invasiveness is not a problem. If harvesting heavily, fertilize with a complete fertilizer in spring and midsummer.

HARVEST: Leaves as needed. Roots in autumn or early spring. Preserve by drying.

OTHER: Use leaves as a potassium-rich mulch around herbs, potatoes, or other plants. Soak comfrey leaves in water for a month to make a high-potassium (but pungent smelling) liquid fertilizer. To speed up the decomposition rate in your compost pile, add comfrey leaves.

USES

FOR HEALTH: Leaf infusion in bath, hair rinses, or in lotions or creams to soften skin and renew cells. Leaf or root poultice, compress, or ointment for sore joints, sprains, varicose veins, bunions, minor burns, wounds, bruises, or hemorrhoids.

CAUTION: Do not take internally.

Besides treating external ailments, comfrey is also a nutrient-rich mulch or compost addition.

Costmary

Tanacetum balsamita

■ **Zone 5**

Costmary was popular during medieval and Elizabethan times for flavoring and preserving beer, strewing on floors, repelling insects, and aiding in childbirth. Early American settlers thought much of its fragrance and often used a leaf as a bookmark in the family Bible, because the leaves dry to a leathery texture. Fresh leaves have a sweet flavor, blending the fragrances of lemon, balsam, and mint.

DESCRIPTION: Perennial, growing as a ground-hugging plant but reaching 3 feet tall and 2 feet wide when in bloom. Bright green, oval leaves to 10 inches long. Clusters of ½-inch, daisylike flowers in late summer. Plants may need staking to stand straight. Can spread quickly by underground runners. Camphor plant (*Tanacetum balsamita tomentosum*) has camphor-scented leaves that are not palatable but are said to repel moths.

Three close relatives of costmary well known for their showy blossoms and insecticidal properties are feverfew (*T. parthenium*), painted daisy (*Chrysanthemum coccineum*), and pyrethrum (*T. cinerariifolium*).

IN THE GARDEN

SITE: Full sun to partial shade. Humus-rich, moist, well-drained soil; pH 6.2. Space 2 feet apart. Plant with their rapid spread in mind. Do not mulch, as runners spread above ground. Containers.

PROPAGATION: Divide in spring or autumn. Difficult to grow from seed (produces little if any seed).

HARVEST: Young leaves as needed. Preserve by drying.

USES

IN THE KITCHEN: Leaves in green or fruit salads, fruitcakes, lemonade, teas, root vegetables, game, or home-brewed beer.

IN THE HOME: Leaves in potpourris or insect-repellents. Leaf infusion for a final rinse for linens.

FOR HEALTH: Leaf infusion internally for colds, indigestion, or cramps; externally in baths, as hair rinse, or facial tonic. Leaf poultice or ointment for insect stings or minor burns.

Costmary (foreground) is also called "Bible leaf" because it was once a popular bookmark for Bibles.

Cowslip
Primula veris

■ **Zone 5**

Cowslips once grew in abundance in the meadows of Europe and England before the era of modern farming. Much folklore surrounds

Grow a large patch of cowslips so you'll have plenty of flowers to enjoy in the garden and with desserts.

these diminutive harbingers of spring, including that they are the keys St. Peter dropped from heaven. They also were purported to preserve beauty in women.

DESCRIPTION: Perennial. Forms a rosette 6 inches across. Crinkled, oval leaves. Leafless stems rise to 9 inches, and are topped by fragrant, yellow bells in early spring.

Common primrose (*P. vulgaris*) is sometimes used interchangeably with cowslip, but there is danger involved in taking it internally.

IN THE GARDEN

SITE: Sun or light shade. Average, well-drained soil; pH 7.0. Space 6 inches apart. Containers.

PROPAGATION: Sow fresh seed in early autumn. Division in late spring or early autumn.

CARE: Control slugs with bait or barriers.

HARVEST: Leaves as needed. Flowers just as they open. Two-year-old roots in spring or autumn.

USES

IN THE KITCHEN: Leaves in green salads. Flowers in desserts, green or fruit salads, or teas. Crystallize flowers for decorating pastry. Flowers also traditionally used to make a wine.

IN THE HOME: Flowers in potpourris.

FOR HEALTH: Flower infusion said to be effective internally for insomnia, nervous tension, allergies, or headaches; externally as facial lotion or ointment for wounds. Root decoction or leaf infusion traditionally used for coughs, colds, as a diuretic, or to slow the blood clotting .

CAUTION: Do not take if pregnant, allergic to aspirin, or taking an anticoagulant medicine such as warfarin.

Coneflower, Purple
Echinacea spp.

■ **Zone 3**

The roots of purple coneflower were an essential medicine for Native Americans of the prairies, and they

No other native American herb has the reputation of echinacea, which stimulates the immune system.

were quickly adopted as a home remedy for colds and flu by the settlers. Besides having antiviral, antifungal, antibacterial, and antiallergenic properties, they also are said to stimulate the body's immune system.

DESCRIPTION: Perennial, growing 2 to 3 feet tall and as wide. Pointed, oval, coarsely toothed leaves 3 to 8 inches long on bristly stems. Daisylike flowers, to 4 inches across, in mid to late summer, with a prominent center of tiny purple florets surrounded by drooping magenta to pink petals.

E. angustifolia, E. purpurea, and *E. pallida* are the species with the greatest medicinal potency. *E. purpurea* and its cultivars, including a white-flowered one, are widely grown as ornamental flowers.

IN THE GARDEN

SITE: Full sun to partial shade. Humus-rich, moist, well-drained soil; pH 6.5. Space 1½ to 2 feet apart. Containers.

PROPAGATION: Seed sown indoors or out in spring. Self-sows. Division in spring or autumn, at least every four years.

CARE: Cut off faded flowers. Pick off Japanese beetles and other insects.

HARVEST: Three-year-old roots after several hard frosts in autumn as plant begins to die back. Replant crown after cutting off the main root.

OTHER: Attracts butterflies; very hardy; good cut flower.

USES

IN THE HOME: Flowers in bouquets.

FOR HEALTH: Root decoction or tincture internally for colds, flu, allergies, or fevers; externally for wounds; as a gargle for sore throats.

Dill

Anethum graveolens

■ **Annual**

Prescribed 5,000 years ago by ancient Egyptian doctors, mentioned as tax payment in the Bible, and included in magicians' spells and lovers' drinks in the Middle Ages, dill is now appreciated mostly for its tangy flavor. It is also virtually synonymous with any form of cucumber pickles.

DESCRIPTION: Annual. Ferny, thread-like, blue-green leaves. Flat, 6-inch clusters of tiny yellow flowers in summer. Flat, oval, light brown seeds. 'Bouquet', 'Hercules', and 'Tetra' grow 3 to 4 feet tall and are slow to flower. 'Dukat' has an especially strong flavor. 'Fernleaf' grows to 18 inches and is especially good for use in containers. Ridged, flattened brown seeds ⅙ inch long.

IN THE GARDEN

SITE: Full sun. Humus-rich, moist, well-drained soil; pH 6.0. Space 10 inches apart. Containers.

PROPAGATION: Sow directly into garden every three weeks from spring until midsummer for a continuous supply of leaves. Self-sows. Plant in fall in hot climates.

CARE: Protect from wind.

HARVEST: Leaves as needed. Cut off flower heads for more fresh foliage. Flowers when fully open. Seeds just as they turn brown. Cut seed heads 2 to 3 weeks after bloom, and hang upside down in paper bags until the seeds ripen, dry, and drop. Preserve by freezing or drying.

USES

IN THE KITCHEN: Leaves (best used fresh) or seeds in soups, salads, cheeses, egg, fish, lamb, pork, poultry, vegetables, apples, vinegars, pickles, sauces, breads, or salt-free herb-seasoning blends.

IN THE HOME: Fresh flowers in bouquets. Dried flowers in wreaths and other crafts.

FOR HEALTH: Seeds after meals to aid digestion and sweeten breath. Seed infusion internally for indigestion, flatulence, hiccups, stomach cramps, insomnia, colic, coughs, colds, flu, or menstrual cramps; diuretic. Dip fingernails in seed infusion to strengthen.

Dill's feathery foliage and airy blooms complement garden flowers as well as flavor food and improve health.

Elder

Sambucus spp.

■ **Zone 3–5**

Stone Age sites show evidence of elder, and the various species of this imposing shrub found worldwide have a venerable history through many civilizations. Over the years, it has been assigned great powers of both good and evil. The roots, stems, and leaves release cyanide, so they should be avoided. The flowers and berries are edible, however, and are used in decoctions and infusions to treat colds, burns, bruises, and many complexion problems.

American elder (*S. canadensis*) grows to 12 feet tall with dark purple berries; zone 3. European elder (*S. nigra*) may reach more than 20 feet tall with purplish black berries; zone 5. Red elder (*S. racemosa*) grows to 12 feet tall with red berries; zone 3. All species are deciduous shrubs, with leaves composed of five to seven oval, pointed, toothed leaflets and dense clusters of fragrant, creamy white flowers in summer. Cultivars are available in variegated, golden- and cut-leaved forms.

IN THE GARDEN

SITE: Full sun to partial shade. Moist, fertile soil; pH 6.5. Space 10 to 20 feet apart.

PROPAGATION: Sow ripe berries outdoors. Semihardwood cuttings in summer. Hardwood cuttings in autumn. Suckers can be dug in spring or autumn.

CARE: Prune in spring and fall to maintain shape and size. For ornamental varieties, cut back almost to the ground.

HARVEST: Flowers when fully open. Preserve by drying. Berries when shiny and purple or red, depending on the species.

OTHER: Attracts butterflies.

USES

IN THE KITCHEN: Flowers in fritters, sorbets, teas, vinegars, or wines. Berries in pies, jellies, jams, or wines. Do not use raw berries.

IN THE HOME: Flowers in bouquets or potpourris.

FOR HEALTH: Flower infusion internally for cold, flu, cough, fever, arthritis, and hay fever; externally in bath, facial tonic, eye compress, ointment for chapped skin; gargle for sore throat. Berries in syrup for cough, decoction for sore joints.

The elder's fragrant flowers hend dark berries are a centuries-old remedy for colds, and they're edible, too.

Elecampane
Inula helenium

■ Zone 3

A bold perennial flower, elecampane has edible roots that are also a remedy for coughs and other ills.

The Roman scholar Pliny reported that the Empress Julia Augusta ate the candied roots of elecampane "to help digestion, to expel melancholy, and to cause mirth." Helen of Troy is said to have been gathering elecampane when she was abducted by Paris. More recent scientific observation shows that the roots contain both antibacterial and antifungal agents.

DESCRIPTION: Perennial, growing 4 to 6 feet tall and 3 feet across. Oval, pointed, bristly leaves to 2 feet long near the base; upper leaves are smaller. Thick, round, woolly stems. Daisy like, yellow flowers to 4 inches across in summer.

IN THE GARDEN

SITE: Full sun to partial shade. Average to humus-rich, moist, clay soil; pH 7.0. Grow in a moist spot if possible. Shelter from wind. Space 3 to 5 feet apart.

PROPAGATION: Seed sown outdoors in spring. Self-sows. Division in spring or autumn, at least every three years to renew the plants.

CARE: Remove faded flower heads.

HARVEST: Two-year-old roots in autumn after two hard frosts. Flowers when fully open. Preserve by drying.

USES

IN THE KITCHEN: Root as a vegetable or a traditional flavoring for sweets.

IN THE HOME: Fresh flowers in bouquets. Dried flowers in crafts. Petals in potpourri. Dried root as incense (has a strong smell of violets).

FOR HEALTH: Root decoction internally for respiratory infections, coughs, or indigestion; externally for acne. Crystallized roots for indigestion or coughs.

Fennel
Foeniculum vulgare

■ Zone 6

The perennial herb fennel differs from the annual vegetable fennel

The versatility of herb fennel extends from the flower garden to the kitchen and medicine chest.

(*F. vulgare dulce*) in that it does not form a white, swollen base. The herb provides fine texture in the garden, a softer, nuttier version of anise in the kitchen, and a gentle remedy for stomachaches.

DESCRIPTION: Perennial, growing to 5 feet tall and 18 inches wide. Threadlike, feathery, blue-green leaves similar to dill. Flat, 6-inch clusters of tiny, edible yellow flowers in midsummer. Oval, ribbed, brown seeds. 'Bronze' or 'Rubrum' fennel has edible, bronze-red leaves; also makes an impressive and imposing plant in the border.

IN THE GARDEN

SITE: Full sun. Average, moist, well-drained soil; pH 6.5. Space 18 inches apart. Containers.

PROPAGATION: Seed sown outdoors in spring.

CARE: According to folklore, fennel should not be planted near bush beans, dill (can hybridize with dill to produce unfavorable seedlings), caraway, tomatoes, kohlrabi, coriander, or wormwood. It is said to adversely affect their growth.

HARVEST: Leaves as needed before flowering. Preserve by freezing. Stems just before flowering. Seeds just as they turn brown.

OTHER: Fennel flowers said to attract beneficial insects.

USES

IN THE KITCHEN: Leaves in salads, fish, pork, eggs, cheeses, beans, rice, or vegetables, butters, or vinegars; add near the end of cooking. Stems in salads or soups. Seeds in sausages, duck, grains, rice, eggs, cheeses, cabbage, sauerkraut, beets, potatoes, breads, butters, or cheeses.

IN THE HOUSE: Fresh flowers in bouquets.

FOR HEALTH: Leaf or seed infusion internally for indigestion, flatulence, or suppressing appetite; externally in facial tonics or steams, gargle for sore throats or mouthwash, or eye compresses.

Feverfew
Tanacetum parthenium
■ Zone 4

Since the time of ancient Rome, feverfew has been an ingredient in sweets and wines, a medicinal for a wide range of ills, and an insect repellent. Only recently has it been asserted that the bitter leaves of feverfew can help relieve migraines.

DESCRIPTION: Perennial, growing 2 to 4 feet tall and 18 inches wide. Many-branched plant with yellowish-green, deeply lobed and divided leaves to 3 inches long. Daisylike white flowers 1 inch across from midsummer to early autumn. 'Snowball', 'White Pompon', and 'White Stars' are double-flowered forms and 'Aureum' has golden leaves, which are not as active medicinally.

IN THE GARDEN

SITE: Full sun to partial shade. Average, well-drained soil; pH 6.3.

Space 1 foot apart. Invasive; set apart from other plants. Containers.

PROPAGATION: Seed sown indoors or outside in spring. Division in spring or autumn. Cuttings in summer.

CARE: Remove faded flowers. Spray aphids and spider mites with insecticidal soap.

HARVEST: Leaves before flowering. Flowers just as they open. Preserve leaves by freezing or flowers by drying.

OTHER: Repels bees; so do not grow near plants that need bees for pollination. Closely resembles chamomile.

USES

IN THE HOME: Fresh flowers in bouquets. Dried flowers in potpourri or crafts. Leaves in moth-repellent mixtures. Leaf infusion as a disinfectant. Flower heads dried or ground for a safe insecticide.

FOR HEALTH: Infusion traditionally taken internally for migraines, tension, arthritis, or insomnia. Eat no more than four small leaves daily. Leaf infusion for facial tonic.

Although used for centuries, only recently has feverfew been considered for treating migraines.

Garlic
Allium sativum
■ Zone 4

Garlic is one of the oldest and most valued of medicinal and culinary herbs. Slaves building the pyramids and Roman soldiers ate garlic to sustain their strength. In Asia, ancient herbalists prescribed it for high blood pressure and respiratory problems. The pungent bulbs are essential to the world's cuisines, enhancing all foods except desserts.

DESCRIPTION: Perennial bulb, composed of four to fifteen cloves, or bulblets, enclosed in a papery tan to pink sheath. Flat, ½-inch-wide leaves growing to 24 inches tall. Small, white to pinkish flowers in round flowerhead in spring to summer. Dozens of cultivars have been bred, varying in clove size, flavor, and keeping quality.

IN THE GARDEN

SITE: Full sun to partial shade. Deep, humus-rich, moist, well-drained soil; tolerates wide pH range. Space cloves 6 inches apart and 2 inches deep. Containers.

PROPAGATION: Pull cloves apart from bulb and plant, pointed end up, in early autumn.

CARE: Winter mulch where temperatures fall below 5° F.

HARVEST: Bulbs when top growth starts to yellow and fall over in summer. Dry and remove tops or braid them. Store bulbs or braids in a dark, cool, airy place. Refrigeration encourages mold.

OTHER: Said to prevent leaf curl on peaches and blackspot and aphids on roses. Infusion as an insect spray. Companion plant for cabbage, eggplant, and tomatoes.

USES

IN THE KITCHEN: Cloves in salads, salad dressings, marinades, stir-fries, stews, beans, soups, beef, lamb, poultry, pork, chicken, vegetables, vinegars, butters, or cheeses; taste can becomes bitter if burned while cooking. Roast whole bulbs.

IN THE HOME: Bulbs on wreaths or braided.

FOR HEALTH: Eat raw or use infusion or tincture internally for cold, flu, respiratory infection, cholesterol cough, diarrhea, bacterial infection, or intestinal parasites. Externally in poultices for insect bites, or cuts; may irritate skin.

The power of garlic is not just in its flavor but also in its ability to fight infections and cholesterol.

Ginger
Zingiber officinale

■ **Zone 9**

More than four hundred centuries ago, ginger from Asia made its way

A tropical herb, ginger is in everything from ginger ale to stir-fries. Also, it's an important remedy.

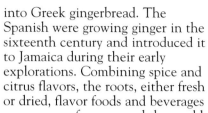

into Greek gingerbread. The Spanish were growing ginger in the sixteenth century and introduced it to Jamaica during their early explorations. Combining spice and citrus flavors, the roots, either fresh or dried, flavor foods and beverages from around the world and are one of the world's favorite medicines, particularly for motion sickness.

DESCRIPTION: Tropical perennial, growing 2 to 4 feet tall. Lance-shaped leaves to 12 inches long and 2 inches wide. Conelike, 3-inch spikes of yellow and purple flowers; usually produced only in warm climates with a long growing season.

IN THE GARDEN

SITE: Full sun to part shade. Humus-rich, moist, well-drained soil; pH 6.5. Containers.

PROPAGATION: Divide rhizomes in early spring; plant horizontally 1 inch deep.

CARE: Maintain even soil moisture. Goes dormant in winter.

HARVEST: Rhizomes in late autumn, cutting off leafstalks and removing fibrous roots. Keep some to start the next year's plants. Peel, cut into 1-inch cubes, and store in vodka in the refrigerator.

USES

IN THE KITCHEN: Fresh rhizome in marinades, stir-fries, drinks, fruit salads, preserves, quick breads, muffins, cakes, cookies, or roast meats; especially with sweet potatoes, winter squash, carrots, beets, pumpkin, rhubarb, or peaches. Crystallized as a sweet or in desserts.

FOR HEALTH: Infusion made from rhizomes for colds, flu, fever, constipation, indigestion, nausea, motion sickness, morning sickness, flatulence, and for poor circulation.

Ginseng
Panax spp.

■ **Zone 4**

The most famous of the Chinese herbs, ginseng has been valued for

Surrounded by a wealth of folklore, ginseng is accepted as a stimulating herb useful for stress.

its therapeutic benefits for more than 7,000 years. Folklore credits it with everything from providing wisdom, long life, and sexual potency, to improving stamina, and resistance to disease. In addition, it is believed to battle about 70 other, specific conditions. Research suggests it may protect against mental and physical stress, increase physical endurance, and assist in maintaining vitality.

DESCRIPTION: Perennial, growing to 18 inches tall. Young plants have one to two leaves, with up to six leaves after three years, each divided into five toothed leaflets radiating from a central point. Clusters of ½-inch green flowers in summer. Bright red berries, each with two to three white seeds.

American ginseng is *P. quinquefolius*, and Asian ginseng is *P. pseudoginseng*. Siberian ginseng (*Eleutherococcus senticosus*) is a related, deciduous shrub growing to 10 feet tall; it has similar properties but is considered to be more stimulating than the others.

IN THE GARDEN

SITE: Partial shade. Humus-rich, moist, well-drained soil; pH 6.0. Space 24 inches apart.

PROPAGATION: Seed difficult to germinate; sow ripe seed in autumn in pots left outdoors or in seedbed; a cold period of four months is necessary for germination.

CARE: Winter mulch. Good drainage is critical to prevent rot. Requires ample warmth and humidity during the growing season.

HARVEST: Five- to seven-year-old roots in autumn. Preserve by drying.

USES

FOR HEALTH: Root decoction or tincture used generally for stress, nervous exhaustion, lack of appetite, or for recovering after an illness or injury.

CAUTION: Do not take ginseng for more than six weeks at a time. Avoid caffeine when taking ginseng; it can result in overstimulation. Do not take when pregnant.

Goldenseal

Hydrastis canadensis

■ Zone 4

Goldenseal is a North American medicinal herb prized by the Cherokee and other native tribes. They used it externally to repel insects and treat wounds, and internally for stomach and liver problems. Astringent and antibacterial properties counter infection and check inflammation.

DESCRIPTION: Perennial, growing to 12 inches tall. Downy, 12-inch-wide leaves deeply divided into five to seven finely toothed lobes. Single, ½-inch, greenish-white flowers in late spring. Orange-red berries with two shiny black seeds.

IN THE GARDEN

SITE: Partial to full shade. Humus-rich, moist soil; pH 6.5. Space 8 inches apart.

PROPAGATION: Difficult from seed, as germination may take two years; sow outdoors in autumn. Division in late autumn when dormant.

CARE: Mulch in summer and winter. Protect from wind.

HARVEST: Three- or four-year-old roots in autumn. Preserve by drying.

USES

FOR HEALTH: Root decoction internally for stress and anxiety, to reduce heavy menstrual bleeding, and to soothe digestive system; externally as an eyewash; gargle for sore throats or infected gums; douche for yeast infections.

CAUTION: Has a cumulative effect and should not be taken to excess. Avoid if suffering from high blood pressure or if pregnant or nursing.

Found wild in North American woodlands, goldenseal roots have a wide range of medicinal uses.

Hops

Humulus lupulus

■ Zone 3

Few herbs are grown on the scale of hops, which are used as a flavoring and preservative in beer. They are also a powerful sedative and have antiseptic properties as well. In the garden, hop vines will readily cover trellises and arbors. They can grow 6 to 12 inches a day, and as much as 30 feet in a year. Because of this, they're often grown as a quick screen on a trellis or arbor.

DESCRIPTION: Perennial vine, growing to 25 feet. Coarse, hairy, 3-inch-long, heart-shaped to lobed leaves with serrated edges. Male and female flowers on separate plants, and both bloom in July and August. Female flowers inconspicuous, maturing into papery green cones. White male flowers in loose bunches several inches long. Many cultivars are grown for beer. 'Aureus' has golden yellow leaves.

Japanese hops (*H. japonicus*) produces hops made into a tonic for treating urinary infections.

IN THE GARDEN

SITE: Full sun. Likes plenty of water. Deep, humus-rich, well-drained soil; pH 6.5. Space 6 feet apart.

PROPAGATION: Seed sown indoors in early spring. Cuttings or suckers in early spring.

CARE: The vigorous vines need ample support and plenty of room to grow. Spray aphids and spider mites with insecticidal soap.

HARVEST: Hops when amber brown and partially dry. Preserve by drying, then refrigerate. Loses effectiveness in six months.

USES

IN THE KITCHEN: Hops flavor beer. Young shoots eaten as a vegetable, either raw or steamed like asparagus. Flowers can be used raw in salads.

IN THE HOME: Hops flowers can be dried to use in wreaths and dried arrangements. Vines for baskets.

FOR HEALTH: Pillow stuffed with hops or hop infusion for insomnia. Hop tincture internally for stress, anxiety, headaches, indigestion, or menstrual pain.

CAUTION: Do not take if suffering from depression.

Hops do more than flavor beer. The shoots can be eaten, and the papery cones readily relieve insomnia.

Horehound
Marrubium vulgare

■ **Zone 4**

Horehound drops or syrups have soothed scratchy throats and coughs

Though associated with cough drops, horehound also helps cure indigestion or stimulate appetite.

with their bittersweet, menthollike quality since the days of ancient Greek physician Dioscorides. One of the ritual bitter herbs of Passover, it also had the reputation of breaking magic spells.

DESCRIPTION: Perennial, growing 2 to 3 feet tall. Bushy plants with woolly stems and leaves. Each serrated, oval leaf to 2 inches long. White flowers in dense whorls in summer. 'Green Pompon' has larger flowers and is particularly useful in bouquets. Woolly horehound (*M. incanum*) is even more woolly and white but is considered an ornamental as opposed to a medicinal plant.

Black horehound (*Ballota nigra*) is toxic in large quantities. It has lavender flowers but is otherwise almost identical to horehound.

IN THE GARDEN

SITE: Full sun. Deep, sandy, well-drained soil; can handle very poor dry soil; pH 7.0. Space 12 to 15 inches apart. Containers.

PROPAGATION: Seed sown indoors or out. Self-sows. Division in spring.

CARE: Cut off faded flowers to prevent self-sowing. Seeds easily and can become a nuisance in the garden. Trim plants in spring to keep them bushy.

HARVEST: Leaves just before flower buds form. The best leaves for harvesting come from the top third of the plant. Preserve by drying and storing in airtight containers.

OTHER: Attractive to bees. Thought to discourage flies.

USES

IN THE KITCHEN: Leaves and seeds in teas, added to iced tea or lemonade, or flavoring for beer.

IN THE HOME: Flowers in dried bouquets and crafts and branches in dried arrangements.

FOR HEALTH: Leaf infusion, syrup, or candy for coughs or sore throats; leaf infusion for poor appetite or indigestion.

Horseradish
Armoracia rusticana

■ **Zone 5**

Allied with beef as a sinus-clearing condiment, horseradish is

The bold, undulating leaves of horseradish top the aggressively growing, multi-purpose roots.

undervalued for its healing properties. It stimulates the appetite and improves digestion and is credited with being a diuretic, mild antibiotic, circulatory stimulant, and hay fever remedy.

DESCRIPTION: Perennial, growing 2 to 3 feet tall and wide. Lance-shaped leaves to 2 feet long and 4 inches wide. Clusters of small white flowers in spring rarely produce viable seed.

IN THE GARDEN

SITE: Full sun. Deep, humus-rich, moist soil; pH 6.8. Space 12 to 18 inches apart. Plant at the edge of the garden to avoid tilling and spreading.

PROPAGATION: Division in spring; any piece of root will grow.

CARE: Locate carefully because it is invasive.

HARVEST: Leaves when young. Roots as needed or in autumn to preserve. Roots have best flavor in autumn. Store roots in sand in a cool, dark place or wash, grate, mix with vinegar or mayonnaise, and refrigerate.

OTHER: Root infusion spray for brown rot on apples.

USES

IN THE KITCHEN: Grated roots with raw beets and sour cream, in slaw, dips, pickled beets, cream cheese, mayonnaise, sauces for roast beef or oily fish. Pieces of roots added to pickles will help keep them crisp. Young leaves in salads.

IN THE HOME: Roots chopped into dog food to dispel worms.

FOR HEALTH: Eat roots raw in food to stimulate digestion or to eliminate mucus and waste fluid during cold, flu, or fever. Roots in cough syrup. Root poultice for stiff muscles.

CAUTION: Overconsumption may irritate gastrointestinal tract. Avoid if have low thyroid function or kidney problems. Avoid continuous large doses when pregnant. Poultice may cause blistering. Avoid touching face or eyes while grating.

Hyssop
Hyssopus officinalis
■ Zone 4

With a strong camphorlike odor, hyssop was strewn throughout musty castles. The minty, bittersweet flavor has long played a role in a wide range of foods, including several commercial liqueurs. In the garden, hyssop brings fine texture and a long bloom period, as well as an attraction for hummingbirds, bees, and butterflies.

DESCRIPTION: Perennial, growing to 30 inches tall and 3 feet across. Sprawling stems with semi-evergreen, small, narrow, lance-shaped leaves to 1 inch long. Spikes of ½-inch, edible blue flowers from summer to early autumn. Pink- and white-flowered forms are available.

IN THE GARDEN

SITE: Full sun to partial shade. Average, well-drained soil; pH 6.7. Space 2 feet apart. Containers.

PROPAGATION: Seed sown indoors or out. Cuttings in late spring or early summer. Division in spring or autumn.
CARE: Remove faded flowers to prolong blooming and encourage bushy growth. Trim in spring and fall to maintain shape. Can be grown as a low hedge or edging.
HARVEST: Leaves as needed; best before flowering. Flowers when three quarters open. Preserve by drying.
OTHER: Said to repel flea beetles and to lure cabbage moths away from cruciferous vegetables.

USES

IN THE KITCHEN: Flowers in salads. Leaves in green or fruit salads, with oily fish, game, lamb, poultry, tomatoes, soups, stews, sausages, fruit pies, or dessert syrups. Combine with mint or lemon balm for herbal tea.
IN THE HOME: Flowers or leaves in potpourri. Fresh or dried flowers in bouquets or crafts.

FOR HEALTH: Leaf infusion internally for sore throat, respiratory infection, poor appetite, indigestion; externally for bath or facial steam. Leaf poultice for wounds and bruises.
CAUTION: Do *not* use medicinally when pregnant.

Hyssop, a beautiful but underutilized herb, has the added benefit of being good for you.

Lady's Mantle
Alchemilla mollis
■ Zone 5

The magical drops of dew that collect in the leaves of lady's mantle were the stuff of alchemist's potions. The perception of it was so powerful that Christians came to identify it with the Virgin Mary and associate it with "women's ailments." Its favor today is mainly based on the beauty it brings to the herb garden.

DESCRIPTION: Perennial, growing to 18 inches tall and 24 inches wide. Bushy plants with deeply folded, velvety, bright green, rounded, 3-inch leaves with scalloped and serrated edges. Open sprays of tiny yellow-green flowers in summer. Plants sold as *A. vulgaris* are usually *A. mollis*; there are more than 200 other species.

IN THE GARDEN

SITE: Full sun or partial shade. Humus-rich, moist, well-drained soil; pH 7.0. Space 2 feet apart. Containers.

PROPAGATION: Seed sown indoors or out. Self-sows. Division in spring or autumn.
CARE: Remove faded flowers. In hot climates, cut back by half in midsummer to stimulate fresh growth.
HARVEST: Leaves as needed. Flowers when fully open. Preserve by drying.

USES

IN THE HOME: Leaves and flowers in bouquets or nosegays.
FOR HEALTH: Leaf infusion internally is said to regulate monthly cycle or provide menopause relief. Also said to ease diarrhea. Externally as facial tonic or steam, especially for large pores or acne, and for lightening freckles; in cream for dry skin; gargle after tooth extraction. Compress for inflamed eyes, wounds, or inflammations.

Appreciated for its lovely leaves and frothy flowers, lady's mantle also has a history as a "woman's herb."

Lavender

Lavandula angustifolia

■ **Zone 5**

Among the most evocative of all fragrances, the sweet, clean scent of lavender brings pleasure to both garden and home. A favorite bath additive of the ancient Greeks and Romans, lavender's name derives from the Latin *lavare,* to wash.
DESCRIPTION: Perennial, growing 18 to 36 inches tall, depending on

Besides offering their distinctive fragrance, lavender flowers also can flavor foods and relieve stress.

the cultivar. Bushy to sprawling plants with small, lance-shaped, greenish-gray leaves. Spikes of lavender flowers in summer; also purple, pink, and white forms. 'Hidcote' and 'Munstead', growing 18 inches tall with purple flowers, are among the hardiest and most popular .

There are many other species and cultivars, including: woolly lavender (*L. lanata*) with velvety, silver-gray leaves, zone 6; fernleaf lavender (*L. pinnata*) with feathery gray leaves, zone 9; French lavender (*L. stoechas*) with large, showy flower bracts, zone 7; green lavender (*L. viridis*) with green flowers, zone 9. Grow tender varieties as annuals.

IN THE GARDEN

SITE: Full sun. Average, well-drained soil; pH 7.1. Space 1 to 3 feet apart. Containers.
PROPAGATION: Seed sown indoors. Cuttings in spring, summer, or early autumn. Layer in late summer.

CARE: Remove faded flowers. Trim in spring to maintain size and shape and to remove dead wood. Do not prune old wood; it will not regrow.
HARVEST: Flowers just as they open. Preserve by drying.

USES

IN THE KITCHEN: Fresh or dried flowers in cakes, cookies, muffins, jellies, black tea, vinegars, fruits, or eggs. Use sparingly or the taste becomes soapy. Crystallize flowers.
IN THE HOME: Fresh flowers in bouquets. Dried flowers in wreaths or other crafts. Moth-repellent sachets. Rub on skin to repel flies.
FOR HEALTH: Flower infusion internally for stress, anxiety, headaches, flatulence, fainting, or bad breath; externally for relaxing baths, facial tonics or creams, or hair rinses, or cold compresses for headaches. Flower oil massaged on skin for muscle or joint pain, insomnia, stress, inflammations, burns, or cuts (may cause dermatitis; don't use at full strength).

Lemon Balm

Melissa officinalis

■ **Zone 4**

A strong fragrance of lemon with a touch of mint makes lemon balm a

Lemon balm is one of the easiest of the "lemon" herbs, but remove the faded flowers to prevent self-sowing.

pleasure to brush against in the garden. A favorite of bees, it in fact gets its name from the Greek word for "bee." It is an excellent tea herb and adds fresh, lemony flavor when sprinkled over cooked vegetables or in fruit salads, and it can function as a milder substitute for lemon verbena.
DESCRIPTION: Perennial, growing to 2 feet tall and as wide. Bushy plant with heart-shaped, scalloped-edged, heavily veined leaves. 'Variegata' is a cultivar with gold-splashed leaves.

IN THE GARDEN

SITE: Full sun to partial shade. Average, well-drained soil; pH 7.0. Space 2 feet apart. Containers.

PROPAGATION: Seed sown indoors. Self-sows. Cuttings in late spring or early summer. Division in spring or autumn.
CARE: Cut back after flowering to prevent self-sowing. Winter mulch.
HARVEST: Leaves as needed. Preserve by drying, but it loses much of its fragrance and therapeutic value.
OTHER: Attractive to bees. Most intense scent when grown in the poorest soils. More tolerant of shade and moisture than most herbs.

USES

IN THE KITCHEN: Leaves in teas, wines, or liqueurs, fish, mushrooms, soft cheeses, dips, or fruit salads. Add at end of cooking.
IN THE HOME: Dried in potpourri. Fresh leaves as furniture polish.
FOR HEALTH: Leaf infusion internally for anxiety, mild depression, nervousness, headaches, insomnia, indigestion, or nausea; externally in lotion or ointment for cold sores, cuts, or insect stings.

Lemongrass
Cymbopogon citratus
■ **Zone 9**

The fresh, lemony taste of lemongrass is an essential element in Southeast Asian cooking, but it can also liven up other foods as well. The leaves provide a relaxing tea and add a lemon fragrance to potpourri.

DESCRIPTION: Perennial, forming a clump to 5 feet tall and 3 feet wide. Long, slender, arching grassy leaves. Blades are sharp-edged and can cut the skin. Rarely flowers except in the tropics.

IN THE GARDEN

SITE: Full sun. Humus-rich, moist soil; pH 6.5. Space 2 to 4 feet apart. Containers.

PROPAGATION: Division in spring or early summer, cutting back to 4 inches. Can be started from a side shoot planted after chance of frost has passed.

CARE: Fertilize monthly during growing season with water-soluble fertilizer.

HARVEST: White leaf base as needed, pulling older, outside stems from base. Freeze short pieces. Cut leaves as needed. Dry in the dark to hold color.

OTHER: Close relative of citronella.

USES

IN THE KITCHEN: Peeled base of the bulbous stem used in a wide variety of Southeast Asian dishes, as well as in stir-fries, soups, pastas, vegetables, curries, or fish.

IN THE HOME: Dried leaves in potpourri.

FOR HEALTH: Leaf infusion internally for indigestion, stress, flatulence, or fevers; externally as poultice for muscle pain.

Grow lemongrass in a pot and bring it indoors during the winter, then summer the plant outdoors.

Lemon Verbena
Aloysia triphylla
■ **Zone 9**

One of the few herbs from South America, lemon verbena is a tropical shrub from Chile. The leaves have a clean, sharp, intensely lemony fragrance and flavor. The essential oil has been used in perfumes since the eighteenth century, when the Spanish took it back to Europe.

DESCRIPTION: Deciduous shrub, growing to 10 feet tall and 8 feet wide. Slender branches with lance-shaped leaves to 4 inches long and ½-inch wide. Open sprays of tiny white and purple flowers in early summer.

IN THE GARDEN

SITE: Full sun. Average, well-drained soil; pH 7.0. Space 3 feet apart. Containers.

PROPAGATION: Seed sown indoors in spring. Tip cuttings in late spring, late summer, or early autumn.

CARE: Bring in container-grown plants before first frost. Plants may drop leaves during winter. In spring, prune to maintain shape and size. Fertilize in containers during the summer. Watch for whitefly or red spider mite infestation; spray with insecticidal soap.

HARVEST: Leaves as needed. Preserve by drying.

USES

IN THE KITCHEN: Leaves in sauces, marinades, salad dressings, teas, drinks, vinegars, fruit desserts, jellies, cakes, or ice creams. Chop leaves finely; they are tough.

IN THE HOME: Leaves in potpourri or infused in candle wax to scent candles.

FOR HEALTH: Leaves in oil for massages, face and hand lotions, and creams. Leaf infusion internally as a sedative tea or for nasal congestion, indigestion, nausea, flatulence, or stomach cramps; externally in bath water for relaxation or in a compress for puffy or irritated eyes.

CAUTION: Long-term use of large amounts of lemon verbena may cause stomach irritation.

Lemon verbena holds its flavor well when cooked, but it must be chopped finely.

Licorice

Glycyrrhiza glabra

■ Zone 5

Besides commercially flavoring candy and stout, licorice roots are a powerful anti-inflammatory. Records of licorice date to 3,000 years ago on Assyrian tablets and Egyptian papyri. The Latin name *Glycyrrhiza* comes from *glykys*, meaning "sweet," and *rhiza*, "root." In fact, one of the compounds in the root called glycyrrhizin is 50 times sweeter than sugar and quenches thirst instead of increasing it.

DESCRIPTION: Perennial, growing to 4 feet tall and 3 feet wide. Large leaves divided into oval leaflets. Spikes of pea-like, purple-and-white, ½-inch flowers in late summer.

Gan cao (*G. uralensis* syn. *G. viscida*) has similar therapeutic qualities and is one of the most important Chinese medicinal herbs.

The roots of licorice are more than candy flavoring. They also help relieve colds and sore throats.

IN THE GARDEN

SITE: Full sun to partial shade. Deep, humus-rich, moist soil; pH 7.0. Plant 3 feet apart.

PROPAGATION: Grows easily from seed. Division in spring or autumn when dormant.

CARE: Grows best with long, hot summers. Invasive; confine roots with a buried barrier. Winter mulch.

HARVEST: Three- to four-year-old roots in early winter. Harvest thoroughly; any piece of root left in the ground will start a new plant; can become invasive in a garden setting. Preserve by drying after peeling bitter bark.

USES

FOR HEALTH: Root decoction or tincture traditionally used for colds, sore throat, constipation, indigestion, or stomach cramps.

CAUTION: Large doses may cause headaches, high blood pressure, or water retention. Do not take if anemic or pregnant.

Lovage

Levisticum officinale

■ Zone 4

Lush and handsome plants, lovage's strong flavor, reminiscent of celery, benefits soups, stews, and roasts. After dinner, lovage tea or liqueur settles an upset stomach. Travelers in the Middle Ages laid lovage leaves in their shoes for the deodorizing and antiseptic effect.

DESCRIPTION: Perennial, growing to 6 feet tall and 2 feet wide. Glossy, deeply divided and toothed leaves on long, hollow stems. Flat clusters of tiny, yellow-green flowers in late summer. Brown, ridged, crescent-shaped seeds ¼ inch long.

IN THE GARDEN

SITE: Full sun to partial shade. Humus-rich, moist, well-drained soil; pH 6.5. Plant 2 feet apart.

PROPAGATION: Seed sown in late summer or early autumn; must be fresh to germinate. Self-sows. Division in spring to early summer. Should be divided every four years.

CARE: To encourage bushy growth, clip off flowers as they appear. Spray aphids with a insecticidal soap.

HARVEST: Leaves as needed. Preserve by drying or freezing. Seeds when ripe in late summer (when they first begin to brown). Two- or three-year-old roots just before flowering.

USES

IN THE KITCHEN: Leaves or stems in green salads, soups, stocks, stews, cheeses, potato salad, rice, stuffing, tomato sauce or juice, or roast meats. Stems or roots cooked as a side-dish vegetable. Seeds, whole or ground, in pickles, biscuits, cheese spreads, salads, salad dressings, sauces, or in herbal seasoning mixes. Leaves and curls from stem for an attractive garnish.

IN THE HOME: Leaves and flowers in bouquets.

FOR HEALTH: Leaf infusion or root decoction internally for indigestion, water retention, menstrual pain, urinary tract infections; externally for wounds. Seeds steeped in brandy with sugar for indigestion.

CAUTION: Do not take medicinally when pregnant or if any kidney function problem is present.

Lovage is a bold, tall ornamental herb well suited for the back of the garden.

Marjoram, Sweet
Origanum majorana
■ Zone 9

Sweet, or knotted, marjoram has a spicy-sweet flavor that is a slightly milder version of its relative, oregano. Women in the Middle Ages put sweet marjoram in nosegays as well as in meat and fish dishes. Medicinally, they knew the advantages of marjoram tea for relieving colds, headaches, and melancholy. Along with oregano and basil, marjoram is considered one of the three main cooking herbs in Italian food.
DESCRIPTION: Tender perennial, treated as an annual, growing to 1 foot tall and 6 inches wide. Velvety oval leaves to 1 inch long on wiry stems. Clustered flower spikes of knotted buds open into tiny pink or white edible flowers in late summer to early fall. Has distinctive knotty green seeds. Hardy majoram, or Italian oregano (*O. × majoricum*), is a similar plant.

IN THE GARDEN

SITE: Full sun. Average to sandy well-drained soil; pH 7.0. Plant 8 inches apart. Containers.
PROPAGATION: Seed started indoors, but germination is slow. Cuttings or layerings in spring or early summer.
CARE: Should be watered sparingly and trimmed often enough to keep the plant in shape.
HARVEST: Leaves as needed or major harvest just before flowering and again before frost. Preserve by drying or freezing.

USES

IN THE KITCHEN: Leaves in salads, cheeses, fish, beef, pork, sausages, tomatoes, cabbage-family vegetables, potato soup, butters, or vinegars. Add near the end of cooking. Throw on grilling coals.
IN THE HOME: Rub fresh leaves on furniture to polish. Dry leaves in potpourri. Dried flowers for wreaths, crafts, or potpourri.

FOR HEALTH: Leaf infusion internally for colds, fevers, coughs, headaches, insomnia, indigestion, painful menstruation, anxiety, or tension; in steam for sinus problems; externally in bath water, hair rinse, ointment or compress for sore or stiff joints, muscular pain, or sprains; gargle for sore throat.
CAUTION: Do not take medicinally if pregnant.

If the flavor of oregano is too strong, try marjoram, which has a milder, sweeter flavor.

Marsh Mallow
Althaea officinalis
■ Zone 3

The spongy cubes of marshmallows no longer have anything to do with this plant, but originally the candy was made with powdered marsh mallow root, water, and sugar. The genus name is from the Latin *altheo*, meaning "I cure," and the mucilage in the leaves, roots, and flowers has soothed since ancient times. Charlemagne was so impressed with this plant that he ordered its cultivation, and the French still eat the tender tops and leaves as a spring tonic.
DESCRIPTION: Perennial, growing 4 feet tall and 2 feet wide. Related to hollyhocks with a similar habit of growth. Velvety, gray-green leaves to 3 inches across, with three to five toothed lobes on woolly, branching stems. Showy, edible flowers, 1 to 2 inches across with five pink or white petals in late summer to early autumn. Round, downy seed capsules contain many flat seeds packed in a circle.

IN THE GARDEN

SITE: Full sun. Average, moist to wet soil; pH 7.0. Plant 2 feet apart.
PROPAGATION: Seed sown outdoors in autumn. Division in spring or fall. Cuttings in spring.
CARE: Cut back by half after flowering.
HARVEST: Leaves as needed, before plants bloom. Two-year-old roots in autumn after heavy frost. Dry leaves or roots or make roots into syrup.
OTHER: Attracts butterflies.

USES

IN THE KITCHEN: Flowers or young leaves in green salads or cooked in soups and stews. In Middle Eastern cuisine, roots are boiled, then fried with onions and butter.
FOR HEALTH: Leaf infusion or root decoction internally for coughs, sore throat, indigestion, or insomnia; externally for dry hands, sunburn, rinse for dry hair, in facial steams, masks, or lotions or in eye compress. Root poultice for drawing and healing. Flower poultice or compress for inflamed skin or minor insect bites. Roots traditionally given to teething babies.

The mucilage in marsh mallow acts as a soothing element for coughs, sore throats, and dry skin.

Meadowsweet
Filipendula ulmaria
■ Zone 4

A favorite strewing herb of Queen Elizabeth I as well as of brides, meadowsweet has leaves with a wintergreen fragrance and flowers with an almond scent. It is most notable for containing salicylic acid, an aspirin ingredient.

DESCRIPTION: Perennial, growing to 2 feet tall and as wide. Dark green, deeply veined, toothed leaves composed of up to five pairs of large leaflets separated by pairs of smaller leaflets. Clusters of small, creamy-white flowers in midsummer. 'Aurea' has golden leaves turning to lime in summer. 'Variegata' has green-and-yellow variegated leaves. 'Flore Pleno' has double flowers.

Meadowsweet has scented leaves and flowers, and it tolerates light shade.

IN THE GARDEN

SITE: Full sun to partial shade. Humus-rich, moist, well-drained soil; pH 7.0. Space 2 feet apart.
PROPAGATION: Seed sown indoors in spring. Division in autumn.
HARVEST: Leaves as needed before flowering. Flowers as they open. Preserve by drying.

USES

IN THE HOME: Fresh flowers in bouquets. Dried flowers or leaves in potpourri or sachets among linens.
FOR HEALTH: Flower infusion used internally for headaches, colds, fever, heartburn, diarrhea, insomnia, or water retention; externally as a facial tonic. Considered one of the best herbal remedies for a wide range of stomach problems, including hyperacidity and heartburn or gastritis.
CAUTION: Do not use if you have a hypersensitivity to aspirin or aspirin products.

Milk Thistle
Silybum marianum
■ Annual or biennial

Milk thistle has been a remedy for liver problems for hundreds of years. The seeds have the highest concentration of the effective ingredient, silymarin, but leaves, flowers, and roots also contain it and are eaten as vegetables. According to legend, the white veins of the leaves carry the milk of the Virgin Mary.

DESCRIPTION: Annual or biennial growing to 4 feet tall and 2 feet wide. Long, narrow, deeply cut leaves with spiny margins and white veins. Magenta-purple flowers in summer. Brown seeds attached to a tuft of white hairs.

A striking, self-sowing ornamental, milk thistle helps remove toxins from the liver.

IN THE GARDEN

SITE: Full sun. Average to humus-rich, well-drained soil; pH 6.5. Space 2 feet apart.
PROPAGATION: Seed sown in spring or autumn. Self-sows.
CARE: Control slugs with bait or barriers. Remove flowers to prolong attractive appearance.
HARVEST: Young leaves as needed. Flowers before they open if eating; after they open if drying. Roots in the autumn. Preserve by drying.

USES

IN THE KITCHEN: Flower head eaten like artichokes. Young leaves in salads or as cooked greens. Roots boiled as a vegetable. (Not primarily used as a food in modern times.)
IN THE HOME: Dried flowers in wreaths and crafts.
FOR HEALTH: Seed infusion aids liver function, helping the liver to renew cells and to combat damage by drugs or chemicals. Historically used as a poison antidote.

Mint

Mentha species and cultivars

■ **Zone 5**

Just as mint spreads throughout the garden, so its flavor and scent have infiltrated cultures down the ages. The Roman scholar Pliny wrote, "The very smell of it reanimates the spirit." That brisk, refreshing taste and aroma permeates our foods, beverages, toothpastes, candies, and chewing gums.

It is the menthol in peppermint and Japanese mint that makes them a beneficial home remedy as well as a flavoring in sweet foods. Spearmint as well as other mints that do not contain menthol are versatile in cooking.

DESCRIPTION: Perennials, growing to 2 feet tall. Oval, pointed, toothed, 2-inch-long leaves in pairs on square stems. Spikes of tiny pink or white flowers in summer. Almost all are very easy to grow.

There are more than 600 species and cultivars of mint.

SPEARMINT: Some of the mints considered best for cooking include Spearmint (*M. spicata*), Austrian mint (*M.* × *gracilis*), curly mint (*M. spicata* 'Crispa'), Moroccan mint (*M. spicata* 'Moroccan'), Vietnamese mint (*M.* × *gracilis*), Bowles' mint (*M.* × *villosa alopecuroides*), red raripila mint (*M.* × *smithiana*), and Kentucky Colonel mint (*M.* × *cordifolia*).

FLAVORED: Other mints with interesting flavors include apple mint (*M. suaveolens*), pineapple mint (*M. suaveolens* 'Variegata'), ginger mint (*M.* × *gracilis* syn. *gentilis* 'Variegata'), chocolate mint (*M.* × *piperita* 'Chocolate'), English mint (*M.* × *spicata* 'English'), grapefruit mint (*M.* 'Grapefruit'), and Hillary's sweet lemon mint (*M.* 'Hillary's Sweet Lemon').

MENTHOL: The mints richest in menthol include field mint (*M. arvensis*), Japanese mint (*M. arvensis* 'Piperescens'), peppermint (*M.* × *piperita*), horsemint (*M. longifolia*), orange mint (*M.* × *piperita* 'Citrata'), and water mint (*M. aquatica*).

GROUND COVERS: Most mints, in fact, are low-growing enough to be tried as a ground cover. Corsican mint (*M. requienii*) has a peppermint scent, grows only an inch tall, and is a good herbal ground cover. It is also considered the least rampant of the mints. Pennyroyal (*M. pulegium*) besides being short enough to use as a ground cover, also has a long history as an insect repellent. Do not take pennyroyal internally.

IN THE GARDEN

SITE: Partial shade but tolerates full sun. Average, moist, well-drained soil; pH 6.5. Plant 2 feet apart. Containers.

PROPAGATION: Division in spring or fall. Cuttings in spring or summer. Seldom comes true from seed.

CARE: Grow in large pots, kept either above ground or sunk up to the rim, to restrain invasive roots, or sink barriers 12 inches into the soil on all sides of the plant. Has a reputation as one of the most invasive plants. Remove flowers to prevent cross-pollination. If rust (a fungal disease) appears, dig up and burn the plant.

HARVEST: Pick only the top tender leaves for cooking; pick as needed. Much better when used fresh. Preserve by drying or freezing.

OTHER: Bees love mint flowers. Can be mowed and will come back vigorously. Mow to new ground every four to five years.

USES

IN THE KITCHEN: Leaves for potatoes, peas, carrots, fruit salads, sauces for meats, jellies, syrups, vinegars, teas and other drinks, or crystallizing. Flowers are edible and good in desserts, cakes, fruit salads.

IN THE HOME: Fresh leaves in bouquets or nosegays, in the bath, sachets, or in cosmetics and soaps. Dried leaves in potpourris. Scatter around food to deter mice. Pennyroyal may deter ants and fleas.

FOR HEALTH: Leaf infusion used internally for indigestion, colds, flu, hiccups, flatulence, or insomnia; externally for chapped skin, rinse for oily hair, facial tonic, or in a refreshing bath.

Mints are widely adaptable, and offer refreshing flavors and a wide variety of products.

The various forms of spearmint are the best for cooking, from vegetables to desserts.

Some mints, such as this variegated pineapple mint, come in flavors ranging from fruit to chocolate.

Myrtle
Myrtus communis
- Zone 9

In ancient Greece, myrtle was sacred to Aphrodite, goddess of love

A traditional herb for wedding bouquets, myrtle can also be trained as topiary.

and beauty, and brides still carry it in wedding bouquets to symbolize love and faithfulness. Although myrtle is a tender plant, it grows well in containers and is often trained as a topiary.

DESCRIPTION: Semi-evergreen shrub, growing to 10 feet tall and 7 feet wide. Small, oval, pointed, glossy, dark green leaves with juniper and orange scent. Fragrant white flowers with golden stamens in early summer. Small purple-black fruit. 'Variegata' has gray-green leaves with creamy-white edges and is not considered as hardy as the species. 'Flore Pleno' has double flowers. 'Microphylla' and 'Microphylla Variegata' both have small leaves and grow to 3 feet tall.

IN THE GARDEN

SITE: Full sun to partial shade. Humus-rich, moist, well-drained soil; pH 7.0. Containers.

PROPAGATION: Seed sown indoors in spring. Cuttings in summer.

CARE: Trim plants in spring to shape and to remove dead or damaged wood. Spray spider mites or scale with insecticidal soap.

HARVEST: Leaves as needed. Flowers as they open. Seed when ripe. Preserve by drying.

USES

IN THE KITCHEN: Leaves with roast pork or lamb or fowl or tossed on coals when grilling. Myrtle berries can substitute for juniper berries.

IN THE HOME: Dried leaves or flowers in potpourri. Leaf infusion for furniture polish.

FOR HEALTH: Leaf infusion considered to be effective when taken internally for urinary infections, vaginal discharge, bronchial congestion, sinusitis, or coughs; externally as an antiseptic wash, facial tonic, compress for bruises or hemorrhoids; ointment for blemishes; gargle for gum infections. Berry decoction as a rinse for dark hair.

Oregano
Origanum vulgare
- Zone 5

The herb that is synonymous with pizza and tomato sauce brings confusion to the garden because there are so many species and cultivars. Also, oregano is sometimes called wild marjoram (sweet marjoram is a close relative). To confuse matters even more, *O. vulgare* often has little flavor. There

The oregano clan's many members, vary greatly in flavor, flowers, and foliage.

are varieties, however, that reliably provide good flavor. Many of oregano's early uses were medicinal, rather than culinary.

DESCRIPTION: Perennial, growing to 18 inches tall and wide. Upright to lax stems with ½- to 2-inch long, velvety, oval leaves. Clusters of ¼-inch edible mauve or white flowers in summer to early autumn.

Flavorful forms of oregano include two species of Greek oregano (*O. vulgare hirtum* and *O. heracleoticum*), also known as winter marjoram, Kalitera (*O.* 'Kalitera'), microphylla (*O. microphyllum*), Syrian (*O. maru*), the compact oregano (*O. vulgare* 'Compactum'), and Turkestan (*O. tyttanicum*). Pot marjoram (*O. onites*) is also called Greek oregano, but is inferior.

IN THE GARDEN

SITE: Full sun. Average, well-drained soil; pH 6.8. Space plants 18 inches apart. Containers.

PROPAGATION: Cuttings in summer. Division in spring or

autumn. Can be unreliable when grown from seed.

CARE: Spray spider mites or aphids with insecticidal soap.

HARVEST: Leaves as needed. Or, for a large harvest, cut back to 3 inches just before flowering and again in late summer. Preserve by drying or freezing.

USES

IN THE KITCHEN: Leaves with salads, cheeses, eggs, tomato sauces, marinated vegetables, roasted and stewed beef, pork, poultry, or game, beans, shellfish, soups, vinegars, pastas, or butters.

IN THE HOME: Fresh flowers in bouquets or nosegays. Dried flowers in wreaths or crafts.

FOR HEALTH: Leaf infusion internally for indigestion, coughs, headaches, or painful menstruation; externally in baths for muscle pain or stiff joints. Flower infusion for seasickness.

CAUTION: Do not use medicinally if pregnant.

Parsley

Petroselinum crispum

■ Zone 5

A ubiquitous garnish, parsley deserves better. After all, the Greek god Hercules chose it for his garlands. It is rich in vitamin C and iron and a natural breath freshener. In cooking, parsley pulls flavors together, with the flat-leaf form being especially flavorful.

DESCRIPTION: Biennial, usually grown as an annual. The curled-leaf form grows 8 to 12 inches tall with finely cut, ruffled, deep-green leaves held on long stems. There are a number of named cultivars. The flat-leaf form grows to 18 to 24 inches tall with bright-green leaves that resemble celery. Flat clusters of tiny yellow-green flowers in spring of the second year of growth.

IN THE GARDEN

SITE: Full sun to partial shade. Deep, humus-rich, moist, well-drained soil; pH 6.0. Space 8 to 12 inches apart. Containers.

PROPAGATION: Seed sown indoors in spring. To speed germination, soak seeds overnight in warm water, then rinse well. Transplant carefully to avoid injuring taproot.

CARE: Grow enough for you and the swallowtail butterfly caterpillar (of which parsley is a favorite). Remove flower heads to prolong growing season.

HARVEST: Leaves as needed. Preserve by drying or freezing.

USES

IN THE KITCHEN: Leaves with salads, sandwiches, eggs, vegetables, meats, soups, stews, roasts, sauces, vinegars, or butters.

IN THE HOME: Fresh leaves in bouquets.

FOR HEALTH: Leaf infusion internally for water retention, urinary infections, indigestion, or mild laxative; externally in poultices or compresses for sprains, wounds, or insect bites; or in hair rinses, facial tonics or steams; or as a lotion for dry skin. Infusion of leaves and stems makes a soothing and cleansing bath.

CAUTION: Avoid medicinal use when pregnant because large doses can irritate the kidneys.

Parsley is a superb, nutrient-rich flavoring that freshens breath as well.

Pink

Dianthus species and cultivars

■ Zone 5

With the genus name translating as "divine flower," pinks have been cherished for centuries for their sweet clove scent and delicate flavor.

DESCRIPTION: Evergreen perennial forming a loose, spreading mat 6 to 12 inches tall. Long, narrow, blue- to gray-green leaves. Fragrant, edible, single or double, white, pink, red, or bicolored flowers on thin, leafless stems in late spring and summer. Numerous cultivars of pinks (*D. plumarius*), clove pinks (*D. caryophyllus*), and cheddar pinks (*D. gratianopolitanus* syn. *D. caesius*).

IN THE GARDEN

SITE: Full sun. Average, well-drained soil; pH 7.0. Space 1 foot apart. Containers.

PROPAGATION: Division in summer after flowering. Layering in late summer. Cuttings in spring. Variable from seed.

CARE: Spider mites may become a problem in areas with long, hot summers; spray with insecticidal soap. Removing flower heads can sometimes prolong blooming. Crown or root rot common if grown in too wet an area.

HARVEST: Flowers as they open. Preserve by drying.

OTHER: Provides nectar for butterflies and bees. Some tendency to self sow if allowed to seed.

USES

IN THE KITCHEN: Remove bitter white heel, then add petals to green salads, fruit salads, fruit pies, sandwiches, vinegars, wines, jellies, or sugar, or crystallize petals.

IN THE HOME: Fresh flowers in bouquets. Dried flowers popular in potpourri.

FOR HEALTH: Traditionally, the petals of pinks in white wine are said to ease stress or tension.

A favorite ornamental, pinks have clove-scented flowers that are flavorful in desserts or drinks.

Rose
Rosa species and cultivars

No flower has stirred people's passions through the ages like the rose. As an herb, rose petals are valued for adding fragrance to potpourri and perfumes, but also play a role in cooking and healing. The fruits, or hips, are a rich source of vitamins, especially vitamin C.

DESCRIPTION: Deciduous shrub, growing from less than 2 to more than 20 feet tall. About 200 species and more than 10,000 cultivars. Leaves composed of pairs of oval, pointed, toothed leaflets on woody, thorned stems. Flowers with five to dozens of petals in pink, red, white, yellow, or orange shades, borne singly or in clusters throughout growing season. Hard to pulpy hips ripen to red, orange, or yellow.

The species and older varieties have the best herbal properties. Consider the white rose (*R.* × *alba*), zone 5; dog rose (*R. canina*), zone 3; cabbage rose (*R.* × *centifolia*), zone 6; damask rose (*R.* × *damascena*), zone 5; gallica rose (*R. gallica*), zone 6; and rugosa rose (*R. rugosa*), zone 2, plus the cultivars of each. Some roses with abundant hips are the dog and rugosa roses; the eglantine rose (*R. rubiginosa*), zone 5; and apple rose (*R. villosa*), zone 5.

Rosa gallica officinalis, **along with the damask rose, was used as a medicine in medieval times.**

IN THE GARDEN

SITE: Full sun. Humus-rich, moist, well-drained soil; pH 6.7. Space 3 to 5 feet apart.

PROPAGATION: Cuttings in autumn or from seed.

CARE: On grafted plants, set the graft union 2 inches below soil level. Prune to shape and remove dead wood in spring. Spray insect and disease pests with neem.

HARVEST: Flowers as they open. Hips when they ripen after flowering. Preserve by drying.

USES

IN THE KITCHEN: Petals, with white heel removed, in salads, teas and other drinks, syrup, sugar, butters, vinegars, fruit pies, cookies, sorbets, or crystallized. Hips in jellies, jams, teas, syrups, or sauces.

IN THE HOME: Fresh flowers in bouquets. Dried flowers in wreaths, crafts, or potpourri.

FOR HEALTH: Petal infusion commonly used externally in facial tonics or dry-skin lotions. Oil infusion for massages is said to aid blood circulation and tone capillaries. Hip infusion or syrup for colds or flu.

Rosemary
Rosmarinus officinalis

■ **Zone 8**

Indispensable in the kitchen, rosemary is steeped in myth, magic, and medicinal uses. Students in Ancient Greece wore rosemary garlands to help them study for exams. It has long been the symbol of remembrance, friendship, and love. Rosemary readily trains as a standard, and in colder climates, it is often grown in pots and brought indoors for the winter.

DESCRIPTION: Woody, evergreen perennial, growing to 3 feet or more tall and as wide; upright forms can reach 5 to 6 feet tall. Gray-green, leathery, resinous, needle-shaped leaves. Edible, pale blue, ¼-inch flowers along stems in spring or early summer. Cultivars with pink, white, or dark blue flowers and forms with trailing growth. The cultivars 'Arp', 'Old Salem', and 'Hill's Hardy' are hardy to zone 6. 'Blue Boy' has compact growth and is ideal for growing indoors.

Add small amounts of rosemary to foods to determine how much you like, as the flavor is intense.

IN THE GARDEN

SITE: Full sun. Average, well-drained soil; pH 7.0. Space 1 to 3 feet apart. Containers.

PROPAGATION: Seed difficult to germinate. Cuttings in spring or late summer. Layering in early summer.

CARE: Trim to shape after flowering. Spray aphids, spider mites, whiteflies, or mealybugs with insecticidal soap.

HARVEST: Leaves as needed. Flowers as they open. Preserve by drying or freezing.

OTHER: Folklore says planting it in the same area as carrots deters carrot fly.

USES

IN THE KITCHEN: Leaves with pork, lamb, poultry, game meats, fish, eggs, cheese, breads, vegetables, pizza, soups, marinades, butters, dried beans, or vinegars. Toss stems on grill or use as skewers. Flowers in salads, sugars, fruit desserts, or crystallized.

IN THE HOME: Dried flowers or leaves in potpourri. Leaf infusion as an antiseptic cleaning solution.

FOR HEALTH: Leaf infusion internally for indigestion or for head colds or sinus congestion; externally in bath water to stimulate circulation, facial steam, or conditioner for dark hair; antiseptic gargle; ointment for sore muscles and joints, bruises, and wounds.

Rue
Ruta graveolens

■ Zone 4

Rue was once thought to cure a wide range of ills as well as to protect against evil. Bunches of rue were used in churches for sprinkling holy water, and both Michaelangelo and Leonardo da Vinci claimed it improved their eyesight. Now it is mainly grown for historical significance as well as for its stunning and unique blue foliage in the garden. Tiny glands over the entire plant release a volatile oil that has a musky fragrance. With its bitter taste and unusual scent, rue is safe to eat, but only in small quantities.

DESCRIPTION: Semi-evergreen, woody shrub, growing to 3 feet tall. Deeply lobed blue-green leaves to 5 inches long. Loose clusters of ½-inch mustard yellow flowers in late summer contrast strikingly with the foliage. Black, crescent-shaped seed. 'Jackman's Blue' has strongly blue foliage; 'Blue Curl' has curled leaves. 'Variegata' and 'Harlequin' have leaves variegated with white.

IN THE GARDEN

SITE: Full sun to partial shade. Average, well-drained soil; pH 7.0. Space 18 inches apart. Containers.
PROPAGATION: Seed difficult to germinate. Cuttings in late summer. Division in spring. Layering in spring or early summer.
HARVEST: Leaves before plants bloom. Seed pods as they ripen. Preserve by drying.

USES

IN THE KITCHEN: Bitter leaves sparingly in salads, sandwiches, cheeses, eggs, or fish. Seed in marinades.
IN THE HOME: Dried stems or seed pods in crafts. Dried leaves in insect-repellent mixtures.
CAUTION: Some people develop a rash much like poison ivy from handling the leaves; wear gloves and long sleeves. Do not use or handle if pregnant.

Rue is known for its ornamental blue-gray foliage, but it also helps repel insects.

Sage
Salvia officinalis

■ Zone 5

The genus name for sage is derived from the Latin word *salvere*, meaning to be in good health, to cure, and to save. Civilizations as diverse as China, Persia, and Europe have attributed many powers to sage. The lemony, camphoraceous fragrance and taste of sage are milder and sweeter when used fresh in cooking. Dried sage dominates food with its musty flavor.

DESCRIPTION: Woody, evergreen perennial, growing to 3 feet tall. Pebbly, gray-green, oval, 2-inch-long leaves. Spikes of edible, tubular, ½-inch, blue flowers in late spring to early summer. There are more than 900 species of sage. Spanish sage (*S. lavandulifolia*), zone 7, and Greek sage (*S. fruticosa*), zone 8, have properties similar to regular sage. The wonderful aromas of the tender perennial (zone 9) fruit sage (*S. dorisiana*) and pineapple sage (*S. elegans*) enhance potpourris, drinks, or desserts. Lyreleaf sage (*S. lyrata*), zone 6, is a native American herb for colds, coughs, or tension. Red sage (*S. militiorhiza*), zone 7, is an important Chinese herb for heart or nerve conditions. Clary sage (*S. sclarea*), zone 4, has a vanilla-balsam aroma; it is both culinary and medicinal.

IN THE GARDEN

SITE: Full sun. Average, well-drained soil; pH 6.4. Space 2 feet apart. Containers.
PROPAGATION: Seed difficult to germinate. Cuttings in late spring or early summer. Layering in spring or autumn.
CARE: Trim to shape after flowering. Replace after five years.
HARVEST: Leaves as needed. Flowers as they open. Preserve by drying (this will affect flavor).

USES

IN THE KITCHEN: Leaves with vegetables, breads, pork, poultry, sausage, stuffings, butters, cheeses, jellies, or vinegars. Flowers in salads, fruit dishes, or teas.
IN THE HOME: Dried leaves in wreaths or insect-repelling sachets. Burn or boil leaves to disinfect a room.
FOR HEALTH: Internally for colds, diarrhea, indigestion, anxiety, tension, coughs, irregular menstruation, menopause; externally for bath, facial tonic, facial steam, rinse for gray hair, or gargle. Rub leaves on teeth to whiten.
CAUTION: Do not take large doses for more than two weeks. Because it contains estrogen, pregnant women should exercise caution with its use.

Fresh sage leaves have a much more pleasant flavor than dried ones. Try them in tomato-based pasta sauce.

St. John's Wort
Hypericum perforatum

■ **Zone 5**

For centuries, St. John's wort has been considered a magical plant, one that could repel evil. A weed that has spread from Britain and Europe around the world, St. John's wort is best known for the treatment of depression, but it also has antibacterial, antiviral, and astringent qualities. The yellow petals turn red when pinched.

DESCRIPTION: Perennial, growing to 2 or 3 feet tall and 1 foot wide. Pairs of small, oval leaves with balsam fragrance on upright stems that spread by sending out runners; the transparent oil glands look like holes. Clusters of bright yellow, fragrant flowers ¾-inch across with five petals and prominent stamens in summer.

When crushed, the flowers of St. John's wort yield a pigment that has medicinal qualities.

IN THE GARDEN

SITE: Full sun to partial shade. Average, well-drained soil; tolerates wide pH range. Space 1 foot apart. Containers.
PROPAGATION: Seed sown indoors in spring. Self-sows. Division in autumn.
CARE: Trim back after flowering to prevent self-sowing.
HARVEST: Flowers as they open. Preserve by drying.

USES

FOR HEALTH: Flower tincture internally for mild depression, anxiety, tension, insomnia, premenstrual syndrome, menopausal problems, cold sores, chicken pox, or shingles. Flower-infused oil externally for minor burns, wounds, bruises, sprains, stiff or sore muscles or joints, hemorrhoids, or minor insect bites.
CAUTION: Prolonged use of St. John's wort may result in skin sensitivity to sunlight.

Salad Burnet
Sanguisorba minor

■ **Zone 4**

Salad burnet is an easily grown but underutilized herb with evergreen leaves high in vitamin C and with a mild cucumber taste. The roots of salad burnet have been used for over 2,000 years in Chinese traditional medicine, although in the West the leaves have had greater importance.

Ornamentally, it is a fragrant, attractive edging for a path, growing best during the cool months of spring and fall. In flavoring, its mild taste combines well with other herbs, especially basil, chervil, dill, tarragon, thyme, and marjoram.

DESCRIPTION: Evergreen perennial, growing to 2 feet tall and 1 foot wide. Mounding rosettes of fern-like stems of 1-inch, oval, toothed leaves. Spherical clusters of red flowers in summer.

Flourishing in the cooler months, the fernlike foliage of salad burnet is best used fresh.

IN THE GARDEN

SITE: Full sun to partial shade. Average, well-drained soil; pH 6.8. Space 1 foot apart. Containers.
PROPAGATION: Seed started indoors in spring. Self-sows. Division in spring.
CARE: Remove flower buds to encourage fresh leaf growth.
HARVEST: Young, tender leaves as needed before flowers open. Roots can be lifted in autumn.

USES

IN THE KITCHEN: Leaves in salads, soups, drinks, cheeses, vinegars, fish, sauces, butters, tomato juice, or vegetables.
FOR HEALTH: Leaf infusion is said to be useful internally for water retention, diarrhea, or hemorrhoids; externally for facial tonic or for minor burns, sores, or sunburn.

Scented Geraniums

Pelargonium species

■ Zone 10

With fragrances of fruits, flowers, spices, and even chocolate, scented geraniums delight the senses. Brought from South Africa in the seventeenth century, they were favored by Victorian women and the French perfume industry.

DESCRIPTION: Tender perennials, growing 1 to 3 feet tall and 1 to 2 feet wide. Velvety leaves, varying from rounded to deeply lobed, plain green to variegated. Edible, pink, deep rose, or white flowers with five petals in summer to autumn. Those most used in the kitchen have the scent of roses or lemons.

IN THE GARDEN

SITE: Full sun to partial shade. Humus-rich, well-drained soil; pH 6.5. Containers.

PROPAGATION: Seed difficult to germinate. Propagates better from cuttings taken in spring, summer, or fall.

CARE: Trim to shape anytime. Pinch growing tips to promote branching. Spray whiteflies or aphids with insecticidal soap. Can be trained as a standard.

HARVEST: Leaves as needed; best fragrance just before flowering. Flowers as they open. Preserve by drying.

USES

IN THE KITCHEN: Leaves in jellies, cakes, cookies, desserts, butters, sauces, syrups, sugars, vinegars, or drinks. Flowers in salads, desserts, or crystallized.

IN THE HOME: Fresh leaves in nosegays. Dried leaves or flowers commonly used in potpourri or sachets.

FOR HEALTH: Leaf infusions used in many external treatments including baths, facial tonics, or facial steams.

Scented geraniums offer a wealth of options, but the favorites are those of rose and lemon.

Soapwort

Saponaria officinalis

■ Zone 3

When boiled, the leaves and stems of soapwort yield a soapy liquid that's gentle for washing delicate fabrics, including antiques, as well as the hair or face. On a summer's evening the flowers exude a scent of cloves and raspberries.

DESCRIPTION: Perennial, growing to 2 feet tall. Oval, pointed leaves to 3 inches long on upright stems, spreading by underground runners. Pink, 1-inch, fragrant flowers in late summer. Double-flowered forms tend to be less invasive.

IN THE GARDEN

SITE: Full sun to light shade. Average, well-drained soil; tolerates wide pH range. Space 2 feet apart.

PROPAGATION: Seed sown indoors or out in spring. Self-sows. Cuttings in early summer. Division in autumn.

CARE: Cut back plants after flowering to encourage a second flowering and to prevent self-sowing. Can become invasive.

HARVEST: Leaves and stems as needed. Preserve by drying.

USES

IN THE HOME: Fresh flowers in bouquets. Boil leaves and stems in rainwater or distilled water for 30 minutes, and strain for washing delicate fabrics, antiques, or anything that requires an especially mild soap.

FOR HEALTH: Boil leaves and stems in rainwater or distilled water for 30 minutes, and strain for washing hair or face; is said to control acne, eczema, or other mild skin problems.

CAUTION: The root is poisonous; do not take internally. Do not grow near fish ponds, because the roots can poison fish.

Even if you never make a soap from soapwort, the fragrant flowers are enchanting in late summer.

Stinging Nettle
Urtica dioica

■ Zone 3

Find an obscure corner of the garden for these weeds with painful,

Goodness comes from the pain of stinging nettle, a nutrient-rich and versatile herb.

stinging leaves. Growing throughout almost the entire United States, they have a long history as a vitamin- and mineral-rich tonic and medicine. Since the Bronze Age, they were also transformed into cloth and provided protection against sorcery.

DESCRIPTION: Perennial, growing to 5 feet tall. Heart-shaped, toothed leaves covered with bristly hairs on stems rising from creeping roots. Loose clusters of tiny green flowers in the leaf axils in summer.

IN THE GARDEN

SITE: Full sun to partial shade. Humus-rich, moist, well-drained soil; tolerates wide pH range. Space 2 feet apart.

PROPAGATION: Seed sown outdoors in spring. Division in early spring.

CARE: Cut plants back to ground in autumn. Can become invasive.

HARVEST: Young leaves in early spring. Roots as needed. Preserve by drying.

OTHER: Attracts butterflies, caterpillars, and moths. Soak plants in rainwater for a week, strain liquid, and use as a spray for aphids or as a high-nitrogen fertilizer. The leaves help speed decomposition in the compost pile.

USES

IN THE KITCHEN: Young leaves, fully cooked, in salads, greens, soups, or teas.

FOR HEALTH: Once a popular spring tonic. Leaf infusion internally for hay fever, asthma, heavy menstrual bleeding, anemia, or water retention; externally in bath to improve circulation, in lotion or cream for itching, eczema, or insect bites, or hair rinse for dandruff or hair loss. Root decoction for enlarged prostate, hay fever, or skin conditions.

CAUTION: Do not eat old plants uncooked. Wear rubber gloves and long sleeves when handling plants. Dock or mullein leaves relieve the sting of nettles.

Summer and Winter Savory

Satureja species

■ Annual, Zone 4

With a peppery, thymelike flavor, savory has enhanced the flavor of

Similar in scent to thyme and marjoram, the two savories can substitute for them in recipes.

food for over 2,000 years. Although the ancient Egyptians incorporated it into love potions, savory's medicinal qualities are more reliably antiseptic and astringent.

DESCRIPTION: Summer savory (*S. hortensis*) is an annual, growing to 18 inches tall and 10 inches wide. Narrow, 1-inch-long, gray-green leaves. White or pale pink ¼-inch flowers in summer. Flavor is sweeter and more delicate than winter savory.
Winter savory (*S. montana*) is a semi-evergreen perennial growing to 12 inches tall and 8 inches wide. Narrow, 1-inch-long, dark-green leaves. Spikes of ¼-inch white to lavender flowers in summer. Strong, more piney than its summer counterpart.

IN THE GARDEN

SITE: Full sun. Average, well-drained soil; pH 6.7. Space plants 10 inches apart. Containers.

PROPAGATION: Seed sown indoors in spring; do not cover with soil. Winter savory also by cuttings in spring.

CARE: Trim plants regularly to encourage new growth. Winter mulch for winter savory.

HARVEST: Leaves as needed. Preserve by drying.

USES

IN THE KITCHEN: Leaves in beans, lentils, soups, eggs, vegetables, sausages, beef, pork, poultry, fish, teas, butters, vinegars, or jellies; popular in salt-free herb blends.

FOR HEALTH: Leaf infusion internally for indigestion, sore throats, coughs, diarrhea, or flatulence; externally in baths, facial tonics, facial steams, insect bites, or mouthwash.

Sweet Cicely
Myrrhis odorata

■ **Zone 3**

Among the few herbs that thrive in shade, sweet cicely forms mounds of lovely, lacy foliage. When cooked with tart fruits, you can use less sugar. The leaves, flowers, seeds, and roots are all edible and highly aromatic. Much like French tarragon, this herb goes especially well with fish, taking away much of the "fishiness". Its size makes it a good choice for the back of the border.

DESCRIPTION: Perennial, growing to 3 feet tall and 2 feet wide. Finely divided, fern-like leaves, velvety on top and whitish underneath, with scent of lovage and flavor of anise. Flat clusters of tiny white flowers which resemble Queen-Anne's-lace in early summer. Shiny, ridged seeds to ¾ inch long, with spicy, licorice flavor. As they ripen, they turn from green to dark brown or black.

IN THE GARDEN

SITE: Partial shade. Humus-rich, moist, well-drained soil; pH 6.5. Space 2 feet apart.
PROPAGATION: Fresh seed sown outdoors in autumn. Self-sows. Division in spring or early summer.
CARE: Needs cold; does not grow in areas warmer than zone 7.
HARVEST: Leaves as needed. Seeds either green or brown. Year-old roots in autumn. Preserve by drying or freezing.

USES

IN THE KITCHEN: Leaves in salads, fish, eggs, soups, stews, butters, vinegars, cookies, cakes, or fruit desserts. Flowers in salads or with fruit. Chopped or crushed seeds in fruit dishes, ice cream, or liqueurs. Roots in salads or as a vegetable, in soups or stews, or infused in brandy.
IN THE HOME: Crush seed for furniture polish. Fresh leaves or dried seed heads in bouquets.

FOR HEALTH: Leaf infusion has been used for coughs, anemia, or indigestion.

A beautiful plant for partial shade, sweet cicely is especially good for flavoring desserts.

Tansy
Tanacetum vulgare

■ **Zone 4**

Once thought to bring immortality, or at least good health, tansy is now known to be toxic. It still has a role in the herb garden and the home for the beauty and insect-repelling quality of its foliage and flowers.

DESCRIPTION: Perennial, growing to 3 feet tall. Feathery, pine-scented leaves on slim stems with vigorously spreading rhizomes. Flat clusters of yellow, button-like, ½-inch flowers in late summer to autumn. Curly tansy (*T. vulgare* 'Crispum') has crinkled leaves and is more compact-growing and less scented. There are also gold- and white-variegated forms.

IN THE GARDEN

SITE: Full sun to partial shade. Average, well-drained soil, pH 6.3. Space 3 feet apart. Containers.
PROPAGATION: Seed sown indoors in spring. Division in spring or fall.

CARE: Cut back after flowering to maintain shape.
HARVEST: Leaves as needed; flowers as open. Preserve by drying.
OTHER: According to folklore, grow near fruit trees to repel insects. Add to compost for its potassium content. Plant near paths to enjoy the fragrance when passing by.

USES

IN THE HOME: Fresh flowers in bouquets. Dried flowers in crafts. Dried leaves or plants around the house to repel flies, ants, or mice.
CAUTION: Do *not* use tansy in any internal medicine or internal treatment.

The leaves of curly tansy can be used to repel insects indoors or out.

Tarragon

Artemisia dracunculus 'Sativa'

■ **Zone 4**

The sophisticated flavor of tarragon, sweet anise with a bite, has made it essential in French cooking. Except

French tarragon is the most popular herb for flavoring white wine vinegar.

for recipes baked in liquid, add tarragon near the end of cooking to prevent bitterness. It blends particularly well with parsley, chervil, garlic, and chives.

DESCRIPTION: Perennial, growing to 2 feet tall and 18 inches wide. Upright to sprawling stems with narrow, pointed leaves to 3 inches long. Tiny, greenish-white, ball-shaped, sterile flowers in summer. Russian tarragon (*A. dracunculus*) produces seed and is much more vigorous, but the leaves are not as flavorful. Mexican mint marigold (*Tagetes lucida*) has a tarragon flavor, withstands summer heat well, and is a fine substitute.

IN THE GARDEN

SITE: Full sun to partial shade. Humus-rich, sandy, well-drained soil; pH 7.0. Space 2 feet apart. Containers.

PROPAGATION: Sterile; rarely blooms; does not produce seed. Division in spring. Cuttings in spring or summer.

CARE: Cut back in autumn and protect with winter mulch. Divide and replant every three years to maintain vigor. Does not grow well in very hot, humid areas. Remove flower heads to keep the plants productive.

HARVEST: Leaves as needed. Preserve by freezing or drying. Also keeps well in vinegar.

OTHER: Believed to enhance the growth of many vegetables.

USES

IN THE KITCHEN: Use with caution, as it is on the bitter side. Leaves in salads, vinegars, cheeses, sauces (especially Bernaise, tartar, remoulade, and hollandaise), salad dressings, mayonnaise, soups, grains, rice, eggs, fish, chicken, pork, butters, liqueurs, vegetables, or pickles.

FOR HEALTH: Leaf infusion, rich in vitamins A and C, iodine, and mineral salts, as a tonic; also stimulates the appetite and aids digestion.

Thyme

Thymus species and cultivars

■ **Zones vary**

The thymes are a profligate group consisting of hundreds of culinary, medicinal, and landscape staples. In cooking, thyme is known as the "blending" herb because it pulls flavors together. It is also known for its antiseptic properties.

DESCRIPTION: Perennial, sometimes evergreen, growing from

Thyme (in the pot) is one of the most versatile herbs for the garden, for cooking, and for health.

1 inch to 12 inches tall. Oval, pointed, ¼-inch-long leaves on wiry stems. Clusters of tiny pink, white, or red flowers in summer.

Common thyme (*T. vulgaris*) grows to 12 inches tall. Forms labeled French or English usually have the best flavor, but variegated forms are also available; also used medicinally; zone 4.

IN THE GARDEN

SITE: Full sun to partial shade. Average, well-drained soil; pH 6.3. Space 8 to 12 inches apart. Containers.

PROPAGATION: Difficult to start from seed. Division, cuttings, or layering in spring.

CARE: Trim in early spring and again after flowering.

HARVEST: Leaves as needed or major harvest just before flowering, cutting plants back to 2 inches. Flowers as they open. Preserve by drying or freezing.

OTHER: Companion plant for tomatoes, potatoes, and eggplant.

USES

IN THE KITCHEN: Leaves in salads, stocks, soups, stews, stuffings, sauces, vinegars, beef, pork, poultry, seafood, sausages, vegetables, honey, butters, cheeses, eggs, rice, grains, breads, or beans. Flowers in salads or as garnish.

IN THE HOME: Fresh leaves or flowers in nosegays or bouquets. Leaf infusion for a household disinfectant. Dried leaves or flowers in potpourri or insect-repelling sachets.

FOR HEALTH: Leaf infusion internally for indigestion, coughs, colds, sore throats, hay fever, insomnia, hangovers, or poor circulation; externally in bath water for muscle or joint pain, insect bites or stings, fungal infections, facial tonics or steams, hair rinse for dandruff, mouthwash, or ointment for minor wounds, sore muscles, or joints.

CAUTION: Do not use medicinally when pregnant or while breast feeding.

Valerian
Valeriana officinalis

■ **Zone 4**

The calming and sleep-inducing effect of valerian has been known since ancient Roman times. A safe, non-addictive relaxant with no "day after" effects, valerian is not related to Valium. The roots have an obnoxious scent. The plants intoxicate cats as catnip does, and the Pied Piper's trick of getting the rats out of Hamelin supposedly involved valerian. Readily naturalizes in northern states, and a beautiful garden plant.

DESCRIPTION: Perennial, growing to 5 feet tall and 3 feet wide. Toothed, fernlike, dark-green leaves. Tall stems with clusters of small, tubular, pinkish white flowers in early summer.

IN THE GARDEN

SITE: Full sun to partial shade. Humus-rich, moist soil; tolerates wide pH range. Space 2 feet apart. Containers.

PROPAGATION: Sow seeds indoors in spring. Self-sows. Division in spring or autumn.

CARE: Remove faded flowers to prevent self-sowing. Divide plants at least every three years to help prevent crowding.

HARVEST: Second- or third-year roots in autumn. Preserve by drying.

OTHER: Planted near vegetables to boost their growth and root decoction sprayed on soil to attract earthworms. Add to compost to increase mineral content.

USES

IN THE HOME: Dried roots or leaves in pillows for cats.

FOR HEALTH: Root decoction or tincture internally for insomnia, stress, anxiety, tension, or badly contracted muscles, adding honey, if desired, to make palatable; externally in baths to calm or lotions for acne or skin rashes.

CAUTION: Don't take in large doses or for more than three weeks.

The flowers of valerian are sweetly fragrant, but the less pleasant smelling roots aid relaxation.

Violet
Viola species

■ **Zones 5, 4**

The diminutive sweet violet (*V. odorata*) and heartsease (*V. tricolor*) have long enamored herbalists, cooks, gardeners, and romantics. The fragrance of the sweet violet is elusive, but the flowers of all violets are a graceful addition to pastries when crystallized. Leaves and flowers of sweet violet and heartsease have medicinal properties. All parts of the sweet violet are edible, it is high in vitamin C, and it is welcomed as a signal of spring. Heartsease, also known as Johnny-jump-ups, was an ingredient in love potions long ago. While still a component of many perfumes, natural extracts of violets have been replaced by synthetics.

DESCRIPTION: Perennial, growing to 6 to 12 inches tall. Often naturalizes. Heart-shaped, dark green leaves. Five uneven petals in shades of purple, blue, violet, pink, yellow, or white, singly or in combination.

IN THE GARDEN

SITE: Prefers partial shade. Humus-rich, moist soil; tolerates wide pH range. Space 6 inches apart. Containers.

PROPAGATION: Seed sown indoors or out in spring. Will self-sow and naturalize.

CARE: Remove faded flowers to prolong flowering. Spray spider mites with insecticidal soap. Grows best in cool weather.

HARVEST: Leaves in early spring. Flowers as they open. Preserve by drying.

USES

IN THE KITCHEN: Flowers in salads, desserts, drinks, syrups, jellies, vinegars, butters, or crystallized. Leaves in salads or infusion in desserts.

IN THE HOME: Fresh flowers in bouquets or nosegays. Dried flowers in potpourri. Pressed flowers in many crafts.

FOR HEALTH: Leaf or flower infusions or root decoctions of sweet violet have been taken internally for coughs, chest colds, or congestion. Leaf or flower infusion of heartsease internally for coughs or bronchitis; externally in bath water, facial tonic, hair rinse, or skin lotion for eczema, dry skin, or itchiness.

Very adaptable and easily grown, sweet violets are diminutive, but have wide-ranging herbal uses.

Woodruff, Sweet
Galium odoratum

■ **Zone 3**

When dried, sweet woodruff has a scent combining vanilla and newly

A deciduous ground cover for shade, sweet woodruff's scent is a mix of vanilla and newly mown hay.

mown hay. This pleasant, calming smell makes it useful for strewing, scenting linen, and stuffing pillows. In the garden, it makes a low-maintenance, deciduous ground cover and appreciates shady conditions. It is essential in the German Mai Bowle, along with Rhine wine and strawberries, and is soaked in white wine to make a beverage called Maitrank.

DESCRIPTION: Perennial, growing to 12 inches tall. Wiry stems with whorls of six to eight narrow, pointed, 1-inch-long, dark green leaves. Small clusters of tiny, starry, white flowers appear in the spring.

SITE: Shade. Humus-rich, moist, well-drained soil; pH 5.5. Space 8 inches apart.
PROPAGATION: Seed difficult to germinate. Propagate by division in early spring.
HARVEST: Leaves as needed. Preserve by drying.
OTHER: Blooms in late spring at the same time as many azaleas and rhododendrons; a useful companion plant beneath them in a woodland or naturalized setting.

IN THE KITCHEN: Leaves used to flavor white wine.
IN THE HOME: Dried leaves and flowers in potpourri, insect-repelling sachets, or wreaths.
CAUTION: Do not take internally, other than occasionally in wine; do not take at all if taking any blood thinners (warfarin, for example) or anticoagulants; contains compounds closely related to these drugs.

Yarrow
Achillea millefolium

■ **Zone 2**

Fossils found in caves suggest that humans have been associated with yarrow in one way or the other for over 60,000 years. Ancient Chinese cast the I Ching with its stalks, Achilles staunched soldiers' wounds with the leaves, and Native Americans employed them for injuries and ailments—just a hint of

Surrounded by centuries of folklore, yarrow has many medicinal uses as well as ornamental forms.

this herb's illustrious medicinal and magical history. Except for the southwestern area of the United States, yarrow grows wild over most of the country.

DESCRIPTION: Perennial, growing to 3 feet tall and 2 feet wide. Fine-textured, feathery leaves to 6 inches long and 1 inch wide on stems spreading by rhizomes. Flat-topped clusters of small white flowers from summer into early autumn.

A number of ornamental cultivars and relatives with flowers in shades of yellow, gold, red, pink, salmon, or peach are available, as are many forms smaller than the species form.

SITE: Full sun. Humus-rich, well-drained soil; pH 6.0. Space 1 foot apart. Containers.
PROPAGATION: Seed sown indoors or out in spring. Self-sows. Divison in spring or fall.
CARE: Remove faded flowers to extend blooming.

HARVEST: Leaves as needed. Flowers when fully open. Preserve by drying.
OTHER: Attracts beneficial insects, benefits nearby herbs, and speeds composting.

IN THE KITCHEN: Young leaves in salads, butters, or cheeses.
IN THE HOME: Dried flowers in wreaths or crafts.
FOR HEALTH: Leaf infusion or tincture internally for colds, flu, fevers, hay fever, arthritis, indigestion, regulating menstrual cycle, heavy menstrual bleeding or pain, high blood pressure, or improving blood circulation; externally in skin lotion, ointment, or poultice for wounds, chapped skin, rashes, or hemorrhoids; gargle for inflamed gums; hair rinse for oily hair. Flower infusion for relaxing bath or facial pack, steam, or tonic.
CAUTION: May cause allergic reaction in rare cases. Do not use medicinally when pregnant.

THE USDA PLANT HARDINESS ZONE MAP OF NORTH AMERICA

Plants are classified according to the amount of cold weather they can handle. For example, a plant listed as hardy to zone 6 will survive a winter in which the temperature drops to minus 10° F.

Warm weather also influences whether a plant will survive in your region. Although this map does not address heat hardiness, in general, if a range of hardiness zones are listed for a plant, the plant will survive winter in the coldest zone as well as tolerate the heat of the warmest zone.

To use this map, find the approximate location of your community, then match the color band marking that area to the zone key at left.

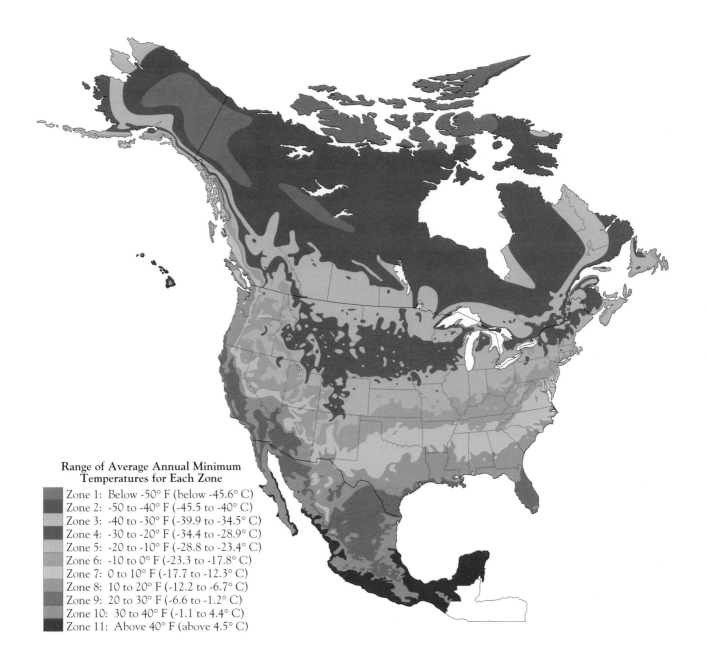

Range of Average Annual Minimum Temperatures for Each Zone

Zone 1: Below -50° F (below -45.6° C)
Zone 2: -50 to -40° F (-45.5 to -40° C)
Zone 3: -40 to -30° F (-39.9 to -34.5° C)
Zone 4: -30 to -20° F (-34.4 to -28.9° C)
Zone 5: -20 to -10° F (-28.8 to -23.4° C)
Zone 6: -10 to 0° F (-23.3 to -17.8° C)
Zone 7: 0 to 10° F (-17.7 to -12.3° C)
Zone 8: 10 to 20° F (-12.2 to -6.7° C)
Zone 9: 20 to 30° F (-6.6 to -1.2° C)
Zone 10: 30 to 40° F (-1.1 to 4.4° C)
Zone 11: Above 40° F (above 4.5° C)

INDEX

Pages numbers followed by t indicate material in tables. Boldface numbers refer to entries in "Choosing Herbs."

METRIC CONVERSIONS

U.S. Units to Metric Equivalents			Metric Units to U.S. Equivalents		
To Convert From	Multiply By	To Get	To Convert From	Multiply By	To Get
Inches	25.4	Millimeters	Millimeters	0.0394	Inches
Inches	2.54	Centimeters	Centimeters	0.3937	Inches
Feet	30.48	Centimeters	Centimeters	0.0328	Feet
Feet	0.3048	Meters	Meters	3.2808	Feet
Yards	0.9144	Meters	Meters	1.0936	Yards

To convert from degrees Fahrenheit (F) to degrees Celsius (C), first subtract 32, then multiply by ⅝.

To convert from degrees Celsius to degrees Fahrenheit, multiply by ⅗, then add 32.